Traverse Theatre Company
with Dundee Rep Theatre

The Grand Old Opera House Hotel

by Isobel McArthur

The Grand Old Opera House Hotel was commissioned by the Traverse Theatre and was first performed at the Traverse Theatre, Scotland, on 27 July 2023.

The Grand Old Opera House Hotel is part of the Made in Scotland Showcase 2023.

Cast
AARON   Ali Watt
AMY   Karen Fishwick

Ensemble
KATHERINE, FRENCH PERSON 1,   Christina Modestou
DRUNK YOUNG WOMAN,
TOREADOR GHOST,
MOTHER WITH BABY,
BRÜNNHILDE GHOST,
BUSYBODY

MORAG, STRESSED GUEST,   Ann Louise Ross
MIDDLE-AGED WOMAN,
SOMBRERO DRINKER,
FASCINATOR WOMAN

YOLANDA, GLASWEGIAN   Betty Valencia
GUEST, FRENCH PERSON 2,
GHOST CARMEN,
WOMAN IN A TOWEL,
TEMPESTUOUS WOMAN

GENERIC STAFF MEMBER,   Laura Lovemore
WOMAN WITH PAINTED NAILS,
YOUNGSTER, SOBER YOUNG
WOMAN, TOURIST,
WOMAN ON A HEN DO,
REGENCY GHOST IN A TALL WIG,
TOREADOR GHOST

PASSING GUEST, BUSINESSMAN,   Barrie Hunter
GHOST FIGARO, MIDDLE-AGED
MAN, MAN IN AN EYEMASK,
HALF-ASLEEP GUEST, MAN WITH
BAD NECK, WORKER IN A HARD HAT

Creative Team

Writer	Isobel McArthur
Director	Gareth Nicholls
Composer & Musical Supervisor	Michael John McCarthy
Set & Costume Designer	Ana Inés Jabares-Pita
Lighting Designer	Lizzie Powell
Sound Designer	Richard Bell
Video Designer	Tim Reid
Casting Director & Vocal Coach	Michael Howell
Movement Director	Emily Jane Boyle
Costume Supervisor	Cleo Rose McCabe
Design Assistant	Caitlin Abbot
Copyist & Musical Director for Recording Sessions	Shonagh Murray

Production Team

Head of Production	Kevin McCallum
Head of Lighting & Sound	Renny Robertson
Lighting & Sound Technician	Dave Bailey
Lighting & Sound Technician	Fi Elliott
Company Stage Manager	Yvonne Buskie
Deputy Stage Manager	Gillian Richards
Assistant Stage Manager	Cécile Pierret

COMPANY BIOGRAPHIES

ALI WATT | AARON
Ali Watt trained at the Bristol Old Vic Theatre School.

Theatre credits include: *Much Ado About Nothing* (Dundee Rep); *Not About Heroes* (Eden Court); *The Stamping Ground* (Eden Court/Raw Material); *Dialogues from Babel and Europe* (Edinburgh International Book Festival); *Richard Gadd: Best Of* (Monkey Barrel Comedy); *Dracula, Far from the Madding Crowd* and *Where Have I Been All My Life?* (New Vic Theatre); *England Street* (Oxford Playhouse); *Blithe Spirit, A Christmas Carol, The Crucible, Heritage, The Monarch of the Glen* and *Perfect Days* (Pitlochry Festival Theatre); *Romeo and Juliet* (Theatre Royal, Bury St. Edmunds); *Country Music* (Trafalgar Studios).

Screen credits include: *The Strange Case of Dr. Jekyll & Mr. Hyde* (National Theatre of Scotland), to premiere at the Edinburgh International Film Festival and screening on Sky Arts in 2023; Irvine Welsh's *Crime* (ITV/Buccaneer Media); *The Cut* (Simon Starling); and *Outlander* (Sony/Starz).

KAREN FISHWICK | AMY
Karen Fishwick has worked internationally in productions including *Our Ladies of Perpetual Succour* (NTS/Sonia Friedman) for which she was Olivier nominated for Best Supporting Actress.

Theatre credits include: *A Christmas Carol* (The Old Vic); *Hansel and Gretel, The Comedy of Errors*, and *Glasgow Girls* (Citizens Theatre); *101 Dalmations* (Regent's Park); *The Caucasian Chalk Circle* (Royal Lyceum Edinburgh); *Wife* (Kiln Theatre); *Romeo and Juliet* and *The Merry Wives of Windsor* (Royal Shakespeare Company); *Hello, Dolly!, The Admirable Crichton, The Yellow on the Broom* and *A Chorus of Disapproval* (Pitlochry Festival Theatre).

Television credits include: *Call the Midwife, The Farm*, and *Badults* (BBC) and *Industry* (HBO).

CHRISTINA MODESTOU | ENSEMBLE
Christina Modestou is originally from Port Talbot, South Wales, and trained at the Arts Educational Schools, London.

Theatre credits include: *Fantastically Great Women Who Changed the World* (UK tour); *Carousel* and *Little Shop of Horrors* (Regent's Park Theatre); *The Boy in the Dress* (Royal Shakespeare Company); *BBC 10 Pieces* (tour); *The Winter's Tale* (National Theatre); *Six* (Arts Theatre); *35MM* (The Other Palace Studio); *Rent* (St James Theatre, UK tour); *The Last Mermaid* (Wales Millennium Centre); *Shrek* (UK tour); *Urinetown* (Apollo Theatre); *In the Heights* (Southwark Playhouse); *The London Revue* (Park Theatre); *Edges* (Tabard Theatre); *Aladdin* (Everyman Theatre); *We Will Rock You* (Dominion Theatre).

Television credits include: *Holy Popcorn* (web series); *Belonging* (BBC Wales); *Strictly Come Dancing* (BBC); *Love Actually*.

Cast albums include: *Fantastically Great Women Who Changed the World, Six The Musical, The Boy in the Dress*.

ANN LOUISE ROSS | ENSEMBLE

Ann Louise Ross has worked extensively in theatre for over 40 years and has been a member of Dundee Rep Ensemble for over 20 years now.

Her previous work for Dundee Rep includes: *Wings Around Dundee, Oor Wullie, The Snow Queen, The Yellow on the Broom, The 39 Steps, Spring Awakening, A Christmas Carol, The Maids, August: Osage County, Death of a Salesman, The Resistable Rise of Arturo Ui, Much Ado About Nothing, Little Red and The Wolf*, and many more. Ann Louise won a CATS Award for Best Female Performance for her role in *Further Than The Furthest Thing*, also with Dundee Rep Ensemble. Ann Louise has worked with the National Theatre and Edinburgh International Festival on a production of *Peer Gynt*.

Ann Louise's television and film credits include: *Trainspotting, The Acid House Trilogy, The Key, The Bill, Rebus, Hamish Macbeth, River City*, as well as numerous radio broadcasts. Ann Louise plays Grannie Island in the hit CBeebies children's story *Katie Morag*, winner of the Scottish BAFTA for Best Children's Programme.

BETTY VALENCIA | ENSEMBLE

Betty Valencia trained at New College Lanarkshire.

Theatre credits include: *Local Hero* (Chichester Festival Theatre); *Orphans* (National Theatre of Scotland); *Cinderella* (Perth Theatre); *We Came To Dance* (Yardheads); *Rapunzel: A Hair Braiding Adventure* (Macroberts Arts Centre); *This Girl Laughs This Girl Cries This Girl Does Nothing* (Stellar Quines/Imaginate); *August: Osage County* (Dundee Rep Theatre).

Film credits include: *The Last Bus*.

LAURA LOVEMORE | ENSEMBLE

Theatre credits include: *The Vagina Monologues* (Dundee Rep); *James IV: Queen of the Fight* (National Theatre of Scotland/Raw Materials); *Much Ado About Nothing* (Bard in the Botanics); *Joke* (Glasgow Oran Mór); *Life is a Dream* (Royal Lyceum Edinburgh); *Panopticon; Scenes for Survival* (National Theatre of Scotland); *I Heart Ice Cream, Shielders, Breakfast Plays, Traverse Young Writers Scratch Nights, Class Act* (Traverse Theatre).

Television and film credits include: *First in Line* (GMAC Films); *The Scotts* (Comedy Unit/BBC); *Death Drop Demon!, Queen of the New Year, How We Forgot to Save the Planet, Trust Me 2, Clique 2* and *The State of It* (BBC); *Sparks* (Very Nice TV); *The Novel* (IWC Media); *Black and Scottish* (Tern Television); *Get Duked* (Feature/Bread Thief Films); and *Only You* (Feature).

Recent radio credits include: *The Servant* (Lepus Productions); and *Rebus* (BBC).

BARRIE HUNTER | ENSEMBLE

Barrie Hunter has worked in Scottish theatre for nearly 30 years, with, amongst others, The Citizens, Scottish Opera, Royal Lyceum Edinburgh, National Theatre of Scotland, The Tron Theatre, Communicado, Mull Theatre, Perth Theatre, Oran Mór & Borderline Companies. He also writes, directs, and performs in panto, and has been Dame at Perth Theatre since 2011.

Recent theatre work includes: *The Stamping Ground* for Raw Material/Eden Court. Previously for Dundee Rep: *Smile, Wings Around Dundee, A-Z of Dundee, Tay Bridge, All My Sons, August: Osage County, Death of a Salesman, The Resistable Rise of Arturo Ui, Love Song, The Cheviot, The Stag and the Black, Black Oil, Witness for the Prosecution, Sunshine on Leith, Gypsy, Macbeth*. Previously for the Traverse: *Welcome to the Hotel Caledonia*.

Television and film credits include: *Karen Pirie, Scots Squad, The Angels Share, Fast Romance, Rab C. Nesbitt, The Field of Blood, Dear Green Place, Still Game, Stacey Stone, Velvet Soup*.

Radio credits include: *Jonathan Watson's Big Society* (Comedy Unit); *Watson's Wind Up* (Comedy Unit/BBC); *Hand in Glove* (BBC).

ISOBEL MCARTHUR | WRITER

Isobel McArthur is an Olivier award-winning playwright and performer.

Theatre credits include: *Kidnapped* (National Theatre of Scotland, 2023); *Pride & Prejudice** (**sort of*) (Tron Theatre, Glasgow and UK tour 2018–2020, Criterion Theatre West End 2022, UK tour 2022–2023); *A Christmas Carol* (Pitlochry Festival Theatre, 2019); *Daphne Oram's Wonderful World of Sound* (Tron Theatre/Scottish tour, 2017); *How to Sing it* (Tron Theatre, 2016).

Awards include: Winner – Olivier Award for 'Best Comedy Play' 2022, Playwrights' Studio Scotland 'Mentored Playwright Award' in 2018 and Tron Theatre's 'Artist In Preview' award in 2016. Nominated – The Stage 'Best West End Debut' 2022, WhatsOnStage 'Best Performance in a Supporting Role' 2021, WhatsOnStage 'Best New Play' 2021.

GARETH NICHOLLS | DIRECTOR

Gareth Nicholls is Artistic Director of the Traverse Theatre.

For the Traverse, his shows include: *Wilf* by James Ley, *Still* by Frances Poet, *Crocodile Fever* by Meghan Tyler, *Ulster American* by David Ireland, *Arctic Oil* by Clare Duffy, *How To Disappear* by Morna Pearson and *Letters to Morrissey* by Gary McNair.

Other productions include: *Kidnapped* by Isobel McArthur (National Theatre of Scotland), *Trainspotting* by Irvine Welsh, *Blackbird* by David Harrower, *Into That Darkness* by Gitta Sereny, *Vanya* by Sam Holcroft (Citizens Theatre); *God of Carnage* by Yasmina Reza, *Under Milk Wood* by Dylan Thomas (Tron Theatre); *A Gambler's Guide to Dying* by Gary McNair (Show & Tell); *Educating Ronnie* by Joe Douglas (Utter).

His work has toured extensively across the UK as well as transferring to Australia, New Zealand, Ireland and USA. Gareth has won numerous awards including four Scotsman Fringe Firsts, three CATS Awards (Critics Awards for Theatre in Scotland) and a Carol Tambor Best of Edinburgh Award.

Previously, he was Main-Stage Director In Residence at the Citizens Theatre, Artist In Residence at Imaginate International Children's Festival and an Emerging Artist at the National Theatre of Scotland.

MICHAEL JOHN MCCARTHY | COMPOSER & MUSICAL SUPERVISOR

Michael John McCarthy is a Cork-born, Glasgow-based composer, musician, and sound designer.

He has worked on over 90 theatrical productions, including ten Scotsman Edinburgh Fringe First award winners, most recently *The Last Return* by Druid Theatre Company. He is also the musical supervisor & co-sound designer on *Pride and Prejudice** (**sort of*), winner of the 2022 Olivier Award for Best Entertainment or Comedy Play.

Theatre credits include: *Ulster American, I Can Go Anywhere, Crocodile Fever, What Girls are Made Of, How to Disappear* (Traverse Theatre); *Kidnapped, The Cheviot, The Stag, and the Black, Black Oil* (National Theatre of Scotland); *The Strange Undoing of Prudencia Hart* (Royal Exchange Theatre); *Little Red Riding Hood, Nora: A Doll's House* (Citizens Theatre); *Cinderella, Tay Bridge, August: Osage County* (Dundee Rep Theatre); *Castle Lennox* (Royal Lyceum Edinburgh/Lung Ha Theatre Company).

His band Album Club released their debut LP on Last Night From Glasgow in May 2022. It reached #6 in the UK Vinyl Albums chart, and #2 in the Scottish Albums chart, spending 6 weeks in the Top 100.

Work for screen includes the documentaries *Where You're Meant To Be* and *Pitching Up*.

ANA INÉS JABARES-PITA | SET & COSTUME DESIGNER

Ana Inés Jabares-Pita is an international, award-winning designer and director working across opera, dance, theatre, fine arts, exhibitions and live music. Her designs are informed by an extensive musical training and fascination with new technologies, magic and illusion.

Previously for the Traverse she designed *What Girls Are Made Of* (UK/International tour), *Letters to Morrissey* and *In Fidelity.*

Theatre credits include: Olivier Award winner *Pride and Prejudice** (**sort of*) (West End/ Criterion Theatre/Royal Lyceum Edinburgh/UK tour); *As You Like It* (Royal Shakespeare Company); *The Lovely Bones* (Birmingham Repertory Theatre/UK tour); *Twelfth Night, Cockpit, Charlie Sonata* (Royal Lyceum Edinburgh); *The Driver's Seat* (National Theatre of Scotland); *Wish List* (Royal Exchange Theatre/Royal Court Theatre); *Lela & Co* (Royal Court Theatre); *The Echo Chamber* (Young Vic Theatre) and *Idomeneus* (Gate Theatre).

Opera and dance credits include: *The Wreckers*, directed by Melly Still (Glyndebourne); *The Flying Dutchman* (Opera Up Close); *BURN* (National Theatre Scotland/The Joyce, NYC); *Breaking The Waves* (European premiere, Theater St Gallen, Switzerland); *Animalis* (Dane Hurst/Dulwich Picture Gallery) and *Remnants* (Print Room/Opera Erratica).

LIZZIE POWELL | LIGHTING DESIGNER

Some of Lizzie Powell's previous lighting designs include: *Cat on a Hot Tin Roof, The Mountaintop, Mother Courage, Anna Karenina, The Mighty Walzer* (Royal Exchange, Manchester); *Macbeth – An Undoing* (Royal Lyceum Edinburgh); *The Comedy of Errors, Endgame, The Libertine* (Citizens Theatre); *James IV: Queen of the Fight, What Girls are Made Of* (Raw Material); *Falstaff* (Scottish Opera/Santa Fe Opera); *A Midsummer Night's Dream* (Scottish Opera); *King John, Macbeth* (Royal Shakespeare Company); *Avalanche: A Love Story* (Barbican/Sydney Theatre Company); *The Da Vinci Code, Dial M for Murder* (Simon Friend Productions); *Our Ladies of Perpetual Succour* (West End/National Theatre Scotland); *Thrown, Orphans, Red Dust Road, Adam, Knives in Hens, Venus As A Boy* (National Theatre of Scotland); *Victory Condition, B, Human Animals, Violence and Son* (Royal Court Theatre); *Our Town* (Regent's Park Open Air Theatre); *Romeo and Juliet* (Crucible Theatre, Sheffield); *Cyrano De Bergerac* (Citizens Theatre/National Theatre Scotland/Royal Lyceum Edinburgh).

RICHARD BELL | SOUND DESIGNER

Richard Bell is a sound designer specialising in theatre sound.

Theatre as sound designer includes: *She Wolf* (Isla Cowan); *Dead Air* (Stockroom); *Fix* (Unbroken Theatre); *Strange Tales* (Grid Iron/Traverse Theatre); *A Table Tennis Play* (Walrus Theatre); *The Ladykillers, Beauty and the Beast* (Theatre by the Lake); *Single Spies* (Theatre by the Lake, York Theatre Royal); *The Game of Love and Chai* (Tara Arts).

Theatre as associate sound designer includes: *The Cherry Orchard* (HOME/Yard Theatre/ETT); *This is Paradise* (Traverse Theatre); *Heroine* (Mary Jane Wells); *The Space Shed* (Unlimited Theatre); *Misty* (Bush Theatre, Trafalgar Studios & The Shed, NY); *My Eyes Went Dark* (59E59, NY); *1984* (London, Australian tour & Singapore International Festival of Arts).

Other media as sound designer: *DOTUS: A US Election Special, The Traverse Theatre Podcast* (Traverse Theatre); *Zombies, Run! Season 1&2* (Six to Start, Android/iPhone app).

TIM REID | VIDEO DESIGNER

Credits include: *Oresteia* (Park Avenue Armory, Almeida Theatre, West End); *Romeo and Juliet* (Cumbernauld Theatre); *The Tsar has his Photograph Taken* (Scottish Opera); *Family Portrait* (Barrowland Ballet); *It Takes All Ten* (Tron Theatre); *Chaplin,The Tramp* (Slovakia National Ballet); *Mary Stuart* (Almeida Theatre, West End); *Macbeth, Quiz, Fracked!* (Chichester Festival); *1984* (Broadway/West End/Almeida/tour); *The Red Barn* (National Theatre); *Show Boat* (Sheffield Crucible/West End); *The Bubbly Black Girl Sheds Her Chameleon Skin* (Theatre Royal Stratford East); *If You Kiss Me, Kiss Me, La Musica* (Young Vic); *Stemmer* (Bergen National Opera); *Scale* (Scottish Dance Theatre); *The Effect, Love Your Soldiers, The History Boys* (Sheffield Crucible); *Quiz Show, Tree of Knowledge* (Traverse Theatre); *Ghost Patrol* (Scottish Opera/Music Theatre Wales); *Clockwork* (Visible Fictions/Scottish Opera); *Girl X, 99... 100, Peter Pan* and *Miracle Man* (National Theatre of Scotland); as Projection Designer: *Wild Swans* (Young Vic/ART).

Tim has worked as Head of Video for the National Theatre of Scotland.

MICHAEL HOWELL | CASTING DIRECTOR & VOCAL COACH

Michael Howell is a Glasgow-based casting director and vocal coach. Recent work as Casting Director includes: *Kidnapped* (National Theatre of Scotland); *Hindu Times* (Edinburgh International Festival); *Oor Wullie* (Selladoor worldwide); *Don Juan* (Perth Theatre); *Still Game: Live* (Phil McIntyre Entertainments/SEE Hydro). For Dundee Rep Theatre: *This is a Love Story, Wings Around* Dundee, *Measure for Measure, A Christmas Carol, The Vagina Monologues, The Steamie* and *Cinderella*.

As Associate Casting Director for James Orange Casting: *Frozen* (Theatre Royal, Drury Lane); *On The Town* (Hyogo Performing Arts Centre, Japan) and *Dr Dolittle* (Music & Lyrics, UK tour).

EMILY JANE BOYLE | MOVEMENT DIRECTOR

Theatre credits include: *Leopoldstadt* (West End/Broadway – Olivier Award for Best New Play, Tony Award for Best Play); *Pride and Prejudice** (*sort of*) (Tron/West End/UK tour – Olivier Award for Best Comedy); *Charlie and the Chocolate Factory, Sunshine on Leith* (UK tours); *Wilf* (Traverse Theatre); *Macbeth* (an *undoing*), *Jumpy, The Lion the Witch and the Wardrobe, Hedda Gabler* (Royal Lyceum Edinburgh); *Exit the King* (National Theatre); *Henry VI, The Mirror and the Light* (Royal Shakespeare Company); *Kidnapped, How to Act* (National Theatre of Scotland); *Measure for Measure* (Shakespeare's Globe); *Oresteia: This Restless House, Lanark* (Citizens Theatre/Edinburgh International Festival); *Trainspotting, Cuttin' A Rug* (Citizens Theatre); *Nora: A Doll's House* (Citizens Theatre/Young Vic); *Muster Station: Leith* (Grid Iron); *Richard III* (Leeds Playhouse); *Talent* (Sheffield Crucible); *Habeas Corpus* (Menier); *A Midsummer Night's Dream* (Regent's Park); *The Return, Not About Heroes* (Eden Court); *Still Game: Live* (SECC Hydro); *The Red Balloon* (National Youth Ballet); *The Cook, The Thief, His Wife and Her Lover* (Faena Theatre); *Tay Bridge, Passing Places, Great Expectations* and *The Cheviot, the Stag and the Black, Black Oil* (Dundee Rep).

Television and film credits include: *The Crown* (Netflix); *Our Ladies* (Sony); *Two Doors Down* (BBC); *In Plain Sight* (ITV); *God Help the Girl* (Barry Mendel/Sigma); *Glasgow Commonwealth Games Opening and Closing Ceremonies* (BBC).

CLEO ROSE MCCABE | COSTUME SUPERVISOR

Cleo is a costume maker, designer and wardrobe technician based in Edinburgh.

She has over 10 years' experience working in costume departments across Scotland, including Royal Lyceum Edinburgh, Dundee Rep Theatre, Scottish Dance Theatre, and the Traverse Theatre. Her design credits include: *Where We Wander* (Hidden Door Festival, 2023); *The Chosen Haram* (Sadiq Ali, Edinburgh Festival Fringe, 2022, international tour, 2023); *Ode to Joy* (Stories Untold Productions, Edinburgh Festival Fringe 2023); *Remedy for Memory* (Stories Untold Productions, 2022).

SHONAGH MURRAY | COPYIST & MUSICAL DIRECTOR FOR RECORDING SESSIONS

Shonagh Murray is a musical director, composer/writer and teacher based in Glasgow. Her most recent MD credits are *A Mother's Song* (Macrobert Art Centre & KT Producing); *Fantastically Great Women Who Changed The World* (Kick Ass Theatre Productions Ltd, Edinburgh Festival Fringe 2022); *Orphans* (National Theatre of Scotland, Associate Music Director); *Bairns in the Woods* (Martin & Martin Productions); *Saturdays Doon The JM* (Dundee Rep Theatre) as well as *SIX: UK Tour* (Global Musicals Ltd, cover MD/Joan). In her work as a composer, Shonagh's children's musical *Nessie* was selected for Capital Theatres and Pitlochry Festival Theatre's New Musical Commissioning Hub 2021, and her musicals *Armour & Burns* both received an award for score composition from Musical Theatre Review (Edinburgh Festival Fringe 2019). As a teacher, Shonagh has lectured at the Royal Conservatoire of Scotland, the London College of Music, as well as guest tutoring at Mountview.

TRAVERSE THEATRE

Here we are – together – marking 60 years of the Traverse. Together, we celebrate six decades of stories that connect, inspire, challenge, entertain and that contribute to the cultural voice of our nation. With an abundance of shows from talented artists with urgent stories that bring life and vitality to our stages – both in-person and digital – the Traverse continues to be a platform for debate, a space for our community, and home of memorable experiences. Across our programme, you can encounter trailblazing creativity that offers unique opportunities to explore the world around us, connect with the lives of others and that spark that vital curiosity in what it is to be human.

The Traverse is a champion of performance, experience and discovery. Enabling people to access and engage with theatre is our fundamental mission, and we want our work to represent, speak to and be seen by the broadest cross section of society. We are specialists in revealing untold perspectives in innovative ways. This is our role as Scotland's premier new-work theatre and a commitment that drives each strand of our work.

Our year-round programme bursts with new stories, live and digital performances that challenge, inform and entertain our audiences. We empower artists and audiences to make sense of the world today, providing a safe space to question, learn, empathise and – crucially – encounter different people and experiences. Conversation and the coming together of groups are central to a democratic society, and we champion equal expression and understanding for the future of a healthy national and international community.

The Traverse would not exist without our overarching passion for developing new stories and embracing the unexplored. We work with bold voices and raw talent – with an emphasis on the Scottish-based – to create the art, artists, and performances that can be seen on our platforms year-round. We invest in ideas and support individuals to push boundaries by placing them at the centre of their own practice, and through artist-led and co-created projects like Class Act and Street Soccer: #SameTeam, we create spaces for stories to take form and grow.

We aim for the timely stories and creative programmes that start life with us to have a global impact, through tours, co-productions, digital life, and translations. We are critically acclaimed and recognised the world over for our originality and artistic risk, which we hope will create some of the most talked-about plays, productions, directors, writers, and actors for years to come.

The Traverse's commitment to bringing new and bold storytelling to global audiences is amplified in Edinburgh each August, when international audiences make the Traverse programme – often referred to as the 'beating heart of the Fringe' – their first port of call in a city overflowing with entertainment offerings.

Here's to the Traverse and all who have created with, played for, visited, and continue to champion everything we are. Our past successes drive our present and future direction, in the knowledge that our unique ability to nurture new talent and engage audiences through ambitious storytelling has never been more crucial in creating and sustaining a vibrant theatre landscape that reflects and challenges the world today.

Find out more about our work: **traverse.co.uk**

With Thanks

The Traverse extends grateful thanks to all of its supporters, including those who prefer to remain anonymous. Their valuable contributions ensure that the Traverse continues to champion stories and storytellers in all of its forms, help develop the next generation of creative talent and lead vital projects in our local community, Scotland and beyond.

With your help, we can write the next scene of our story. Visit **traverse.co.uk/support-us** to find out more.

Individual Supporters

Diamond
Alan & Penny Barr
Katie Bradford
Kirsten Lamb
David Rodgers

Platinum
Judy & Steve
Angus McLeod
Iain Millar
Mike & Carol Ramsay

Gold
Roger & Angela Allen
Carola Bronte-Stewart
Iona Hamilton

Silver
Bridget M Stevens
Allan Wilson
Gaby Thomson
Chris & Susan Gifford
Lesley Preston
John Healy

Bronze
Barbara Cartwright
Alex Oliver
    & Duncan Stephen
Patricia Pugh
Beth Thomson
Julia & David Wilson
Stephanie & Neil
Drs Urzula
    & Michael Glienecke
Viv Phillips
Jon Best & Kate Duffield

Trusts, Foundations and Grants

Anderson Anderson & Brown Charitable Initiative
Arnold Clark Community Fund
Backstage Trust
Baillie Gifford Community Awards
British Council Scotland and Creative Scotland: UK in Japan 2019–20
Bruce Wake Charitable Trust
Cruden Foundation
D'Oyly Carte Charitable Trust
Dr David Summers Charitable Trust
Garrick Charitable Trust
Harold Hyam Wingate Foundation
Heritage Fund
Idlewild Trust
John Thaw Foundation
Murdoch Forrest Charitable Trust
Museum Galleries Scotland
RKT Harris Charitable Trust
The David and June Gordon Memorial Trust
The Foyle Foundation
The Great Britain Sasakawa Foundation
The JMK Trust
The JTH Charitable Trust
The Leche Trust
The Mackintosh Foundation
The McGlashan Charitable Trust
The Nancie Massey Charitable Trust
The Nimar Charitable Trust

The Noël Coward Foundation
The Paul Hamlyn Foundation
The Robert Haldane Smith Charitable Foundation
The Robertson Trust
The Royal Edinburgh Military Tattoo
The Russell Trust
The Teale Charitable Trust
The Turtleton Charitable Trust
The William Syson Foundation
The W M Mann Foundation Theatres Trust
Unity Theatre Trust
Visit Scotland

Traverse Theatre Production Supporters

Cotterell & Co
Paterson SA Hairdressing

Grant Funders

The Traverse Theatre is funded by Creative Scotland and The City of Edinburgh Council. The Traverse has received additional support from the Scottish Government's Performing Arts Venue Relief Fund and Adapt and Thrive, part of the Scottish Government's Community and Third Sector Recovery Programme and delivered in partnership by Firstport, Corra Foundation, SCVO, Just Enterprise, Community Enterprise and Social Investment Scotland.

In Residence Partners

The Traverse has the support of the Peggy Ramsay Foundation / Film 4 Playwrights Awards Scheme.

The Traverse Theatre is further supported by IASH, the Institute of Advanced Research in the Humanities, the University of Edinburgh.

Challenge Project

The Traverse Theatre is currently participating in Creative Informatics' Challenge project as one of the Challenge Holders.

Creative Creative Informatics supports individuals and organisations working across the creative industries in Edinburgh and South East Scotland to develop new products, services and businesses using data and data-driven technologies. The programme is delivered by the University of Edinburgh, in partnership with Edinburgh Napier University, CodeBase and Creative Edinburgh.

Creative Informatics is funded by the Creative Industries Clusters Programme managed by the Arts & Humanities Research Council with additional support from the Scottish Funding Council. It is also part of the City Region Deal Data-Driven Innovation initiative.

Traverse Theatre

Dave Bailey — Lighting & Sound Technician
Linda Crooks — CEO & Executive Producer
Marcin Dobrowolski — Customer Experience Manager
David Drummond — General Manager
Fi Elliott — Lighting & Sound Technician
Jennifer Galt — Creative Engagement Producing Assistant
Jenny Gilvear — Producing & Programme Coordinator
Ellen Gledhill — Director of External Affairs
Robbie Gordon — Creative Development Director
Becca King — Administration & Finance Assistant
Michelle Mangan — Publicist
Kevin McCallum — Head of Production
Anne McCluskey — Senior Creative Producer
Luke Morley — Production & Projects Coordinator
Gareth Nicholls — Artistic Director
Conor O'Donnelly — Marketing Manager
Julie Pigott — Director of Finance & Operations
Pauleen Rafferty — Payroll & HR Manager
Renny Robertson — Head of Lighting & Sound
Serden Salih — Digital Content Associate
Lauren Scott — Marketing & Media Assistant
Gordon Strachan — Ticketing & Data Manager

Also working for the Traverse

Debbie Bentley, Stacey Brown, Eve Buglass, Ruth Cawthorne, Rachel Clinton, Lyra Cooper, Stephen Cox, Ian Cunningham, Leni Daly, Katie Edmundson, Sandra Ferrer Garcia, Roe Fraser-High, Elise Frost, Avril Gardiner, Noa Gelb, Laura Gentile, Jazmin Gilham, Bee Hayes, Darren Hunsley, Jessica Innes, Amandine Jalon, Sam Johnston, Jonathan Kennedy, Lana Kirk, Hannah Low, Mollie MacGregor, Becks Marnie, Zoe Maunder, Matt McBrier, Alison McFarlane, Olivia McIntosh, Jack MacLean, Sophie Malcolm, Abbie Meldrum, Danny Menzies, Tiger Mitchell, Afton Moran, Ellie Moran, Nathaniel Morley, Chris Mundy, Aude Naudi-Bonnemaison, Dan Nelson, Chloe Park Robertson, Zoe Robertson, Gabriele Schena, Eva Shaw, Staci Shaw, Lev Slivnik, Rob Small, Heidi Steel, Colin Sutherland, Eve Thomson, Odhran Thomson, Jessica Wain, Dominic Walsh, Maritza Warnik, Katrine Widell, Rocky Williams, Alice Wilson.

THE GRAND OLD OPERA HOUSE HOTEL

Isobel McArthur

2

Characters

AARON, *thirties. A naturally open book, trying hard to stay closed and just fit in. Struggles to hold down a job for long. Easily distracted. Nervous. Never worked in a hotel before*

AMY, *thirties. Worked in hotels for a few years. Practised in presenting a cheery disposition. Secretly an opera fan but never actually been to see one. Big brain and heart – but scared of putting herself out there. Talks to herself a lot – eccentric*

MORAG, *a hotel worker for her whole life. Zero aspirations to anything more. Working-class background. Seen it all. A bit spiritual – got perspective*

KATHERINE, *assistant manager at the hotel – aspirations to become manager. Slightly neurotic*

YOLANDA, *a hotel worker for several months, Colombian – highly intelligent and academic. Finds all those about her embarrassing. Deadpan*

GENERIC STAFF MEMBER, *wide-eyed. Couldn't hurt a fly*

PASSING GUEST
GLASWEGIAN GUEST
YOUNGSTER
STRESSED GUEST
WOMAN WITH PAINTED NAILS
FRENCH PERSON 1
FRENCH PERSON 2
BUSINESSMAN
MAN IN AN EYEMASK
SOBER YOUNG WOMAN
MIDDLE-AGED MAN
MIDDLE-AGED WOMAN
DRUNK YOUNG WOMAN
HALF-ASLEEP GUEST
TOURIST

WOMAN IN A TOWEL
MOTHER WITH BABY
COUPLE HAVING SEX
MAN WITH BAD NECK
TEMPESTUOUS WOMAN
FASCINATOR WOMAN
WOMAN ON A HEN DO
BUSYBODY
WORKER IN A HARD HAT

And other GUESTS *and* GHOSTS…

Multi-rolling

ACTOR 1 – Aaron

ACTOR 2 – Amy

ACTOR 3 – Katherine, French Person 1, Drunk Young Woman,
Toreador Ghost, Mother with Baby, Brünnhilde Ghost, Busybody

ACTOR 4 – Morag, Stressed Guest, Middle-Aged Woman,
Factory Worker Ghost, Sombrero Drinker, One Half of Couple
Having Sex, Fascinator Woman

ACTOR 5 – Yolanda, Glaswegian Guest, French Person 2,
Ghost Carmen, Woman in a Towel, Tempestuous Woman

ACTOR 6 – Generic Staff Member, Woman with Painted Nails,
Youngster, Sober Young Woman, Factory Worker Ghost,
Tourist, Sombrero Drinker, One Half of Couple Having Sex,
Woman on a Hen Do, Regency Ghost in a Tall Wig

ACTOR 7 – Passing Guest, Businessman, Ghost Figaro,
Middle-Aged Man, Man in an Eyemask, Toreador Ghost,
Half-Asleep Guest, Man with Bad Neck, Worker in a Hard Hat

Stuff to Know

There's at least one surtitle screen which shows translations of anything either inaudibly quiet, very fast, or sung/spoken in a language other than English. In this script, these surtitles appear in square brackets:

CHARACTER. Come questo. [Like this.]

There's a digital screen to show the relevant room number near or above the hotel-room door in the set – quite large. This can change at any time. In this script, these are written centrally, like this:

273

The Set

A hotel room with a corridor alongside, a door adjoining them. In the room, a barely double bed, wardrobe, window, bleak wee space with a kettle, some other basic furniture and a door, leading to an en suite, off. In the corridor, no plants, no art – one bin.

Room and corridor both some lifeless colour.

This text went to press before the end of rehearsals and so may differ slightly from the play as performed.

To begin with, all is in half-darkness.

Then – a swell of non-musical sound. GUESTS *moving suitcases, the shunting of a lift, chattering and other commotion through the thin walls. This is not a place of rest.*

Lights up on the corridor. Evening, for now.

624 625 626 627 628 629

AARON *entering down the corridor. He wears a beige room attendant's uniform with a small backpack. He looks flustered and disorientated. A* PASSING GUEST *(a real bastard) with a wheelie suitcase appears.*

PASSING GUEST. You – could you help me?

AARON *thinks.*

AARON. I don't know.

AARON *sets off –*

PASSING GUEST. Excuse me – where are you going?

AARON. To my staff training, I'm running late –

PASSING GUEST (*flying off the handle*). Is this how you treat loyal customers – ?!

AARON. Oh no I didn't mean to –

PASSING GUEST (*brandishing a card*). I have been a Scomodo Hotel Group Platinum Points Member for eleven years!

AARON. I'm sorry. I mean, congratulations.

AARON *sets off again.*

PASSING GUEST. Who is your manager?

AARON (*fast, distracted*). That's the thing. I'm not sure. It's my first day. Well – almost. First there's more training. Then tomorrow I start properly. Officially. In the morning. You don't know where room two-eight-three is, do you – ?

PASSING GUEST. You want *me* to give *you* directions – ?

AARON. That would be *so kind* – I really can't be any later. Because I'm not entirely sure what else I can try if I'm no good at this. It's so hard finding a job, let alone keeping one – I've not slept in weeks! Everyone says I need to work on my people skills –

PASSING GUEST. Listen – !

AARON. Yes! You're right – it's important to be a good listener – must listen, listen, listen –

PASSING GUEST. To me! – I'm checking out now but my flight's not till ten p.m., can I leave my suitcase at reception?

Beat.

AARON. I wouldn't know.

PASSING GUEST (*incensed*). You just deliberately wasted my time, didn't you?!

AARON. No, I swear – !

PASSING GUEST. Have you any idea what even *one minute* of my time is worth compared to yours? – I mean, what do they even pay you here?!

AARON. Um well – there are benefits. The room attendants all live on site, so even though it's minimum wage, you don't have to worry about rent or anything and once you've paid off the cost of your uniform it's actually not too –

PASSING GUEST. You can't even answer a straight question, can you?

AARON. Yes. I mean – no. Wait – which one am I – ?

PASSING GUEST. Oh shut up! Since it's your first day, I've got a tip for you –

AARON (*putting his hand out*). That's awfully kind –

PASSING GUEST. Not that kind of tip!

Get this straight: we want our sheets changed, our carpets hoovered and our bins emptied. You have *nothing* to say that anyone wants to hear. No one – and I can't stress this enough – no one cares how you 'feel'.

Beat.

AARON. So –

PASSING GUEST. So – shut it!

The PASSING GUEST *marches off.*

AARON (*to himself*). Of course.

The lights flicker above AARON*'s head in the corridor. He looks up. Then – a noise is coming from inside one of the rooms – the door to it opens just an inch or two with a creak. Light escapes.*

There is the distant sound of singing. AARON, *intrigued, approaches the door tentatively.*

A beautiful, female voice singing 'Silver Moon', Rusalka.

THE VOICE.
**Rekni mu, stribmy mesicku,
me ze jej objima rame**

**[Silver moon, tell him
Mine are the arms that shall hold him]**

Standing in the corridor, AARON*'s eyes widen. He cannot discern the language but the meaning is clear. A hand through time. It is heartfelt and human and yet – ethereal. As if reaching him from another dimension.*

AARON (*whispering reverently*)....Wow.

As if by its own volition, the door then opens wide. Inside the room, the silhouette of a female form, obscured but magnificent, backlit, surrounded by smoke, brandishing something. She sings out –

AARON *is captivated. He wants to cry. The tenderness of it is debilitating.*

THE VOICE.
Mesicku, postuj chvili
reckni mi, kde je muj mily
Ohhh – !

[Moon, stay here a while
And tell me where is my beloved…]

Just at that moment –

Fizzz!

Aaaaaah!

All singing out. Sparks fly overhead – ! The main light has short-circuited, plunging the room into almost total darkness.

AARON. Aaaaaaah!

Completely overawed, AARON *runs from the room, out the door and down the corridor.*

The lights flicker again then recover. The figure emerges through the doorway and is revealed to be a young woman in a room attendant's uniform. She has large red headphones over her ears and is holding a toilet brush. She wafts away the smoke, removes her headphones, looking down the corridor.

AMY. Hello?…

Then up at the smoking fixture.

Exploding lights now as well, is it? You'd think Othello was arriving on his ship. No warning, no prelude – bang! (*Laughing to herself.*) Mad decision, really, Verdi! Making everyone shit themselves before the opera's even started!

She glances up again, suddenly forlorn –

But then… I think even a crackpot like you would have packed this job in by now.

She stares. It's too sad. Too real. She puts her headphones back on before returning to cleaning.

A swell of non-music hotel noise. Lift, bustle, people, muffled chatter…

The corridor –

(*No numbers on the room doors.*)

A woman, MORAG *– stands in the corridor in an ill-fitting room attendant's uniform, staring into space.*

Her fingers are poised as if holding a cigarette. She takes it to her lips to smoke it. Then does a double take.

MORAG. Oh, now… where's my fag gone?

She looks around. No sign of it.

Ah well –

She lights another. A younger woman, KATHERINE, *marches purposefully down the corridor. She wears a suit and has an iPad on a holster. Between her index finger and thumb, an incriminating lit cigarette, presented in the manner of an irate headteacher.*

KATHERINE. *Why* am I holding this?

MORAG (*jumping*). Oh! Good question! Didn't think you were a smoker?

KATHERINE. *I'm asking* – why are there lit cigarettes on the floor – ?

MORAG. Must be one of the guests –

KATHERINE. It was you.

MORAG. I'm more or less off the tabs these days.

MORAG *takes a drag on her current cigarette.*

Oh, you mean this? No – I found this on the carpet, too, actually. Just getting rid of it. Terrible business. Fags on the flair? This is a 'no smoking' hotel… S'a disgrace, someone should be fined –

KATHERINE. *Bin!*

The light fixture above their heads flickers.

(*Glancing up.*) Not that one, as well? I don't understand, it's new wiring…

KATHERINE *stares at the lighting fixture whilst* MORAG *takes both fags, has a last big drag on each and bins them.* AARON *appears, running down the corridor, breathless and wide-eyed with revelation.*

(*Eyes on her iPad list.*) Here for staff training?

AARON. Am I? Oh, yes I suppose I am! I forgot about that.

KATHERINE. You're late.

AARON. Well I was told to go to two-eight-three but it doesn't exist.

KATHERINE. *This* is two-eight-three.

AARON *looks at the room-number screen. It's blank.*

AARON. How are you supposed to know?

KATHERINE (*with heavy sarcasm*). How? Well there's this little knack to it, you see – it might not have occurred to you, but you *read the number off the* – Oh, for goodness' – !

MORAG. The Digital Age! What d'you think, son? Installed these screen thingies six months ago. Half of them are already broken.

KATHERINE *is investigating the problem, swiping at her iPad.*

KATHERINE. It's just teething problems.

000 000 000 000 000 000

MORAG. It's unnatural. Having all these wires… The *soul* of this building's Victorian.

AARON. The outside does look old.

MORAG. That's why the locals call it The Grand Old Opera House Hotel –

KATHERINE. They do not. They call it The Scomodo Hotel
Station Road Central.

MORAG (*unconvinced*). Oh aye, right enough. (*Gesturing her
disagreement to* AARON.) Well they've taxidermied the
place.

AARON. I don't understand.

MORAG. They've ripped its guts out and stuffed it with plastic
crap. This all used to be… (*Casting an eye about, reverently.*)
gold and red velvet and those wee binoculars you got… Now
look at it.

(*All blank again.*)

KATHERINE. *Now* it's hi-tech…! (*Losing patience with the
screen.*) Bloody thing…!

AARON. Sorry – this used to be an opera house?

MORAG. Aye. Well, a long time ago. S'been changing hands
for years… These Scomodo people finally bought it and
turned it into a hotel.

The screens recover.

283 284 285 286 287 288

It's fucking ugly, isn't it?

KATHERINE (*seeing the screen*). Thank God.

AARON. So do you ever play opera music here or – ?

KATHERINE. Why would we do that?

AARON. It's just – I honestly don't know where to begin
explaining this but –

KATHERINE. This is a contemporary space. No one's
interested in opera. The shell would have stood here
crumbling for *another* hundred years if Scomodo hadn't
saved it. Now, it's got multiple internal storeys, spotless new
interiors – that's the genius of their work: to stand here, you
wouldn't know this place was ever a dusty old theatre at all.

AARON. No, you really wouldn't.

KATHERINE *shoots* AARON *a look. Was that sarcasm?*

I didn't mean –

KATHERINE. You'd do well to just listen and learn today.

AARON. Of course. That's what I'll do.

Beat. MORAG *stares at* AARON.

MORAG. Something wrong with you, son? You look like
you've seen a –

YOLANDA. Staff training?

YOLANDA, *the uniformed woman from earlier, has
appeared.*

KATHERINE. Through here.

KATHERINE *opens the door with a keycard. She gestures –*
MORAG *and* YOLANDA *file in.*

The room is revealed as AARON *enters.*

(*Checking her iPad.*) Who am I missing…?

YOLANDA *is slumped against a wall,* MORAG *makes
herself comfortable on a small chair,* KATHERINE *stands
by the door checking the names on her iPad –* AARON
stands awkwardly dead-centre.

MORAG (*to* AARON). What's your name anyway, son – ?

AARON. Aaron.

MORAG. I'm Morag.

AARON. That's not what it says there.

MORAG. What?

AARON. Your name badge, it says 'Danielle'.

MORAG (*casually*). Oh right, aye. I've got a few different
ones. Lose track of which I'm wearing. I dropped 'Morag'
down the toilet in my first week. The rules say 'full uniform
with name badge' so, as long as you've got one, it doesn't
matter what it says.

AARON *looks at* YOLANDA.

AARON. Is she wearing the wrong name, too?

MORAG. Couldn't tell you. We don't get to socialise. Rushed off our feet every shift! Changing sheets, answering buzzers. You won't see anyone! Well – apart from all the bloody guests.

The lights flicker above them. Only AARON *seems to notice. A* GENERIC STAFF MEMBER *walks through the still-open door.*

KATHERINE. You're late!

A silly negotiation ensues whereby space must be made for them. Lots of apologising, inappropriate proximity and awkward contortion.

Just find somewhere to put yourselves, will you! We have to run to time. (*Slavishly following her iPad script.*) The Scomodo Hotel Group have requested team meetings at this branch to try and tackle some problems we're having with communication. (*Following her iPad script.*) So, we need to ask: what's at the heart of the issue – ?

GENERIC STAFF MEMBER. Nothing works properly –

MORAG. And the guests are all moody bastar–

KATHERINE. That was a rhetorical question, actually, thank you. (*iPad.*) Now, for some, there might be a language barrier. You… (*Reading name badge.*) 'Dave' – ?

YOLANDA. Yolanda.

KATHERINE. Yolanda, yes. Is that the case for you? That there's a language barrier?

YOLANDA. No.

KATHERINE. Oh dear, you maybe aren't following me… Case in point I suppose. The point is – (*Returning to her corporate script.*) for many people communication is a real weakness.

MORAG. Talking's not my weakness!

KATHERINE. Talking isn't the same as –

MORAG. Shortbread! I've got a real weakness for that –

KATHERINE. That's not –

MORAG. And Tia Maria. And pies!

GENERIC STAFF MEMBER. Mine's exams. Failed them all.

MORAG. Failing them can actually be a sign of very high
intelligence. I failed mine. Hated school! (*Raising her voice*.)
I bet you hated school too, Yolanda, eh?

YOLANDA. Well, in Colombia I did a Masters in Biomedical
Pharmacological Science.

MORAG. Did ye?

Beat.

That sounds nice.

KATHERINE (*iPad*). Let's try an exercise.

*The lights flicker again, much more pronounced now. This
time everyone looks up to examine them.*

GENERIC STAFF MEMBER. Is someone coming to look at
the lights?

KATHERINE. It's all being investigated. We'll have a report in
a month or so. (*Returning to the iPad*.) Now, can we focus?!
We need someone to play a room attendant uhm – Yolanda –
(*Insistently*.) this will benefit you the most. (*Raising her
voice*.) *Little English lesson*.

YOLANDA (*shuffling reluctantly to the centre of the room*).
Qué porquería…

[Such bullshit…]

KATHERINE. And we need someone to be a customer with
a complaint –

MORAG. I'll do that!

MORAG *and* YOLANDA *come forward and stand opposite
each other.*

KATHERINE. Fine – Morag, you're a guest. You've called the
room attendant to your room – Yolanda, go outside – knock
on the door, then show us how you resolve the issue.

YOLANDA *tries to open the door to the corridor but can't.*

GENERIC STAFF MEMBER. Door's stuck.

MORAG. Is it really necessary to use the door for this – ?

KATHERINE. Yes – *here* – !

KATHERINE *opens the door with some force and her keycard, 'beep-beep!'* YOLANDA *exits.*

And – action!

YOLANDA *knocks.* MORAG *pulls at the door.*

MORAG. Stuck again.

KATHERINE. Oh, for goodness' – !

KATHERINE *opens the door again and the pair stand in the room. For different reasons, they are both terrible actors.*

YOLANDA. Hello.

MORAG. Hello. I have a complaint.

YOLANDA. What is your complaint?

MORAG. Well, my door's fucked for a start.

KATHERINE. Something else!

MORAG. Fine, fine… Ehm… why is everything in this hotel the same colour?

YOLANDA *considers this.*

YOLANDA. I suppose you'd have to put it down to a kind of… cultural homogenisation under capitalism. That misguided, corporate belief that designs like these which court the Aesthetically Unspecific – in all their rejection of ornament, history or narrative – risk offending no one. When in reality such places disturb, imprison and unsettle nearly everyone.

MORAG (*trying to stay in character*). Well – what are you going to do about it?

YOLANDA. What can I do about it? I wash bedsheets for a living. Goodbye.

YOLANDA *goes to leave and the door catches her finger –*

Aah! Son of a bitch!

GENERIC STAFF MEMBER (*spotting* YOLANDA*'s hand*).
She's bleeding!

MORAG (*with misplaced conviction*). An injury! From *my door*? This hotel is a deathtrap, I want my money back!

KATHERINE. No one move! Yolanda – stem the flow! We cannot get a *speck* of blood on this carpet – ! Get some toilet paper, will you – (*Straining her eyes at the badge.*) Mohammed – ?

GENERIC STAFF MEMBER (*not moving*). My real name's actually Sarah –

KATHERINE. Forget it! Yolanda – just get in the en suite! (*Spotting the tea tray.*) Morag, on your knees and check the carpet –

MORAG. You can't talk to paying customers like this!

KATHERINE. You're not in character now, Morag! Everyone – this is imperative. Each room must look brand new.

MORAG. That's impossible, Katherine, it's a hotel.

KATHERINE. Yes. And it must feel like *no one has ever stayed here before*. The furniture straight, the surfaces – clear. The bedsheets – a perfect c–

GENERIC STAFF MEMBER. Shit – !

KATHERINE *has pulled back the duvet – revealing a pair of red knickers in the sheets. She grabs the knickers and holds them up.*

KATHERINE. Somebody's… *scants*?

YOLANDA *re-emerges, intrigued, a big wheel of bloody toilet paper around her hand.*

This room is supposed to be guest-ready! Were any of you responsible for cleaning it?

Everyone looks at their shoes.

Then I will check the system, identify the staff member and they *will* be sacked – !

MORAG. No!

KATHERINE. Was it you?

MORAG. No! – I mean, yes, okay it was me who cleaned it but about the knick-knocks – I can explain!

KATHERINE. Go on then – !

MORAG feels the eyes on her.

MORAG. Logically, this can only be…

Everyone leans in, tense –

The work of the supernatural.

KATHERINE. Save it –

MORAG. A ghost!

AARON. Wait – what? Ghost?

KATHERINE. There is no such thing as –

MORAG (*authoritatively*). I put on fresh sheets this morning. No one else has entered the room! It's clear. These undercrackers came from The Beyond!

GENERIC STAFF MEMBER. I never even knew ghosts wore lingerie.

KATHERINE. Yolanda – *you* don't believe this?

MORAG begs YOLANDA with her eyes.

YOLANDA (*unconvincingly*). I couldn't rule it out.

KATHERINE (*exacerbated*). Madness…!

MORAG. Katherine, I wish I could agree with you. I really wish I could – but the pants speak for themselves. Now, we've all had a fright with this ghost business and, personally, I'd just like to get back to my cleaning –

KATHERINE. Not so fast, Morag. (*To* AARON.) You.

AARON. Yes?

KATHERINE. You don't buy this, do you?

AARON looks deeply worried.

AARON. Like you say, it's probably better if I just listen today and –

KATHERINE. No. I'm asking for your opinion, now. I want to know exactly how you feel about all of this.

Panic –

MORAG. / He's hardly had a moment to catch his breath – !

GENERIC STAFF MEMBER. You can't expect him to know after one / day – !

KATHERINE. Even so!

Everyone falls silent –

Be completely honest with me – have you seen *anything* to suggest that this hotel is 'haunted'?

AARON. Well…

The staff all lean in imploringly.

Beat.

(*Totally earnest.*) Yes because I saw a ghost myself.

Theatrical gasps. MORAG *punches the air behind* KATHERINE*'s back.*

KATHERINE. *What?!*

MORAG. First day and he's already seen one!

KATHERINE. Nonsense! *Where – ?*

AARON. In one of the rooms, earlier –

KATHERINE. But what do you mean, 'ghost'? What did it look like?

MORAG. Don't bombard him with questions, Katherine, he's probably still recovering – !

GENERIC STAFF MEMBER. Brave man, so brave –

AARON. It was… a woman.

More gasping.

MORAG. Yes! (*Grabbing the pants again.*) That's Her!

KATHERINE. A woman? So what? That could have been anyone.

MORAG. Did she… (*Feigning a saintliness.*) Have a message for you, son? From over yonder?

AARON. She was…

AARON *physically changes with the thought of it –*

Singing.

GENERIC STAFF MEMBER (*brow furrowed in sympathy*). You must have absolutely shat it, mate.

AARON. It was scary but – I also think it might have been the most wonderful thing that ever happened to me.

MORAG. You do know, Aaron, why the opera house shut down in the first place? There was a fire! They say that the singers who died in the blaze can still be heard.

AARON. Oh God. Do they really say that?

MORAG. They do!

KATHERINE. Who's 'they'? Nonsense!

MORAG (*laying it on thick*). There's a presence here. I've always sensed it.

GENERIC STAFF MEMBER. Is that why you took a job here, Morag?

MORAG. No. Best Western gave me the sack.

KATHERINE. Enough! This place is completely, one hundred per cent, ghost-free.

Bang! The en suite door slams shut suddenly.

AARON. Aah – !

Buzz! GENERIC STAFF MEMBER *looks at a buzzer on her belt – it's flashing and vibrating – an alarm sounds followed by:*

AUTOMATED VOICE. Scomodo Team Member – it is time to begin your shift.

GENERIC STAFF MEMBER. Katherine, my buzzer's going. I need to start.

KATHERINE *looks at her watch.*

KATHERINE. Go! Everyone, go. (*To herself.*) This has been a monumental waste of time… (*To* AARON.) Not you. Wait here. I need to grab you a buzzer and a name tag. But don't touch anything – please. I'll need to do a full inspection of this room later.

GENERIC STAFF MEMBER, KATHERINE *and* YOLANDA *exit,* MORAG *starts checking the space for any other objects.*

MORAG. Don't mind me, son – just having a wee inspection myself.

MORAG *pulls out the under-bed drawer. There's a big inflatable sex doll.*

A-ha.

AARON (*utterly innocent*). Is that… the work of the supernatural, too?

MORAG (*deadpan*). No. That's someone's manky old sex doll that I've not had time to bin.

AARON *tentatively picks up the red pants – then looks at* MORAG *with the doll.*

AARON. Wait, you weren't… (*Innocently.*) fibbing? About these?

MORAG. Oh no, son, no! I'm as honest as the day is long.

AARON. So how can you tell what's supernatural and what isn't?

MORAG. Well ehm… there's a knack to it.

AARON. What kind of a… 'knack'?

As if well-practised, MORAG *bites the doll, then forces out the air, starting to fold it up. Hisssss…*

MORAG. If you think about it – they're bright red! The colour of blood! Of passion!

MORAG *leans in to try and really freak* AARON *out.*

And the colour… of the flames that engulfed those poor singers!

The lights above their heads flicker –

AARON (*disturbed*). Oh God, of course…

MORAG. You'll find plenty of your own surprises on your rounds, I'm sure.

AARON. It's really that common?

MORAG. Pet, sometimes we have eight minutes to do the sheets, carpets, en suite, desk – *the lot*. It's inevitable. Just, if you're checking someone in, try and hide anything that's been missed before the guests notice.

AARON. Right.

MORAG *walks to the door.*

I'll see you around then?

MORAG. Oh I wouldn't have thought so…

MORAG *exits enigmatically.* AARON *looks at the empty room. Noise bleeds in from rooms adjoining. A large beautiful moon can now be seen shining bright in the sky. Almost supernatural-looking… At that moment, the light overhead shoots sparks out and short-circuits. Darkness.*

AARON. Aaah!

In his panic, AARON *tries the door. It's stuck. He rattles it in his frame –*

Hello! Hello – can someone let me out?

Lights up on the corridor. The woman from earlier, big red headphones around her neck, approaches the door from the other side.

AMY. Hello? Are you okay?

The lights recover.

AARON. Is that you, Katherine?

AMY. No... Who's there – ? The guests in this room are supposed to have checked out yesterday.

Racket from an adjoining room – like a cartoon bar brawl. Yelling and smashing.

AARON. I'm Aaron, I work here! Almost.

AMY. What?

Noise abates a little.

AARON. I said I work here!

AMY. Oh! Do you want to just open the door, then?

AARON. I can't – it's stuck.

She tries from outside. No luck.

AMY. It's like *Bluebeard's Castle*, isn't it? 'What's behind the door?' 'More creepy shit covered in blood? – Oh there's a surprise! – *Not!'*

AMY *laughs heartily.* AARON *is baffled.*

Beat.

AARON. Sorry... what?

AMY *(embarrassed).* Of course. Sorry. Never mind. I'll just go and find someone to let you out –

AARON. No, can you explain it to me, please? What's Bluebell's – ?

AMY. *Bluebeard's Castle*. It's an opera. With a lot of locked doors.

AARON.…opera?

Beat.

She can't resist –

AMY (*fast, enthusiastic*). So – ! There are these newly-weds. And he's a bit weird 'cause he's lived in a castle all his life. Anyway, once they get married she's thinking 'Right, s'pose I'll be moving into the creepy castle too, then!' And they go there and she's like, 'Let's crack a window, open these doors, get a bit of daylight in here' and he freaks out 'No! Please! I haven't had time to tidy up!' and she's like 'What did you think was gonna happen? We just got married – ! Obviously I'm opening your doors.' So she does and some of the things behind the doors – and there's really no getting around this – some of them are *really weird* but she says 'You know what, Bluebeard' – that's his actual name – she says, 'Bluebeard, thank you for letting me in. Okay, it wouldn't have killed you to run the hoover around but I'm glad I'm looking behind your doors. Because this is who you really are. And whatever happens…

I love you.'

A couple of beats. Both feel something.

(*Coy.*) It think it's a metaphor or –

AARON (*also embarrassed*). Right, right.

AMY *tries the door again. She glances up at the door number.*

AMY. 'Two-eight-three'. This door's always getting stuck, actually.

AARON. Oh – do you work here, too?

AMY. Oh sorry – yes! I work here.

AARON. I've only just started.

AMY. Me too!

AARON. When?

AMY. Well, a few years ago. But I'm definitely about to leave.

AARON. Oh.

AMY. Soon.

She falters.

It can't be –

This is a stopgap.

AARON. Right.

The longer I live… (*Sincerely.*) The more convinced I am that my whole life, to date, has been one enormous stopgap.

Beat – AMY *looks endeared to him.*

(*Concerned by the silence.*) Sorry – that was way too intense – ! I don't know what I was thinking. I always talk too much. I'm so boring!

AMY. No! It's okay. I like talking.

AARON. …really?

AMY. I don't meet many people who say what they're really thinking.

AARON. Oh I do that a lot.

AMY. So… what are you really thinking right now?

AARON *goes to speak – bangs and crashes from above.*

AARON. Is it always this noisy?

AMY. 'Fraid so. Well – I mean – this is Friday night. Friday night's like bloody… *Turandot*!

AARON. That's – ?

AMY. Puccini. Lots of drums.

AARON. You're really into classical music?

AMY. Yeah. Well, opera. It's the only reason I took a job here. The history… The ghosts.

AARON *starts*.

AARON. You know about the ghosts, too?

AMY. Yeah. I love these old opera houses –

AARON (*trying and failing to act casual*). What… what do you know about it, exactly?

AMY. It's such a sad story. The last time this was a functioning opera house, they were rehearsing a brand-new work by Bernazetti – *I Innamorate Fenici*.

   [*The Phoenix-Like Lovers.*]

AARON. 'Eee-minamm…' You say that… really well. What's the story of that opera then?

AMY. Classic love story – fall for each other, circumstances keep them apart; right at the end: die in each other's arms. Well – *so we think*! All copies of the libretto were destroyed in the fire.

AARON. So there was a fire?

AMY. Oh yeah. It was all documented. In 1923 – sorry – you probably don't want to listen to any more of my –

AARON. No! Please!

   I want to listen to you.

   AMY *hears this*.

AMY. Okay.

   (*Passionately.*) In 1923, the opera house was losing money. So, they started operating as a cinema by day whilst the singers rehearsed. Only, one afternoon, the projector caught – the place went up in flames.

AARON. And people died?

AMY. The audience escaped but the singers got trapped. The two leads were in love in real life, apparently. The story goes, they kept singing their final duet even as the flames engulfed them.

AARON *looks disturbed*.

AARON. And, all these singers, you think they might… still be here?

AMY *smiles*.

AMY. Do you?

AARON. I mean, honestly, I've never really thought about ghosts before. But then today – and you're going to think I'm mad –

AMY. I won't –

AARON. And laugh at me –

AMY. I would never –

AARON. But today I think I might have seen one. I was walking past one of the rooms… the door was open – enough for me to hear something and I don't really know why but… I stayed to listen. Suddenly there was this woman. Standing in the doorway. The lights had gone so I couldn't quite – it's hard to describe to someone who wasn't there…

AMY (*imploringly*). Try.

AARON. She was small, one hand on her hip…

AMY *looks down at her hand resting naturally on her hip*.

She wearing something on her head, I don't know…

AMY *feels for her headphones* –

She looked… magical.

AMY *blushes*.

AMY. Do you think she saw you?

AARON. No. She was in some kind of trance.

AMY. A trance?

AARON. Well…

AARON *collapses to the floor under the weight of this memory. He's beaming.*

She was singing.

AMY *looks mortified –*

AMY. Oh God…

AARON. And this voice she had…

AMY (*cringing hard*). Oh God, oh God no, listen –

AARON. I know, it sounds crazy.

I mean I barely have the words to describe this singing voice to you –

Awful noise kicks in again, they speak quickly over one another, forced to shout –

AMY. / I'm so embarrassed. It's just a hobby! No – not even a hobby – what am I saying? I just tried it. For a joke! It was a joke. I know I'm not any good or anything –

AARON. I'm not great with words at the best of times, there are usually too many or not enough, you know? But to describe this… do the words even exist?!

Noise abates suddenly –

(*Still yelling.*) *All I know is that was the single most beautiful sound that I ever heard!*

Beat.

AMY *looks up from her hands.*

AMY. You're joking?

AARON. I haven't been able to stop thinking about it. I feel… different. Hearing her – I think it rearranged my atoms, you know? You've not heard her, have you? The ghost?

AMY. Well –

AARON. Of course. You would know if you had – ! That voice…! If you'd heard it you'd be in love with it, too!

AMY....love?

AARON beams. AMY doesn't know what to say.

AARON. Hello? Are you still there?

AMY. I'm here.

AMY is now sitting, too. They both speak tenderly into the door.

AARON. I knew exactly what she was...

Because I feel like that.

All the time.

Beat. AMY closes her eyes. She knows exactly.

So... what do you think? Am I mad?

AMY. No.

AARON. Was it real?

AMY (*tenderly*). Yes.

Urgency –

AARON. I need to hear her sing again. Summon her? A séance? Oh I don't know – but this means something, it has to.

AMY. It does!

AARON. Do you think there's a way to find her?

AMY. Yes. I know how!

AARON. Really?

AMY. I'll just go and get my keycard –

AARON. Don't go – !

AMY. I need to get through this door –

AARON. Katherine will be back in a minute, I think – !

AMY. It won't take me long. Anyway, I really need to see your face –

AARON. Please – could you just tell me now? How can I find her again?

AMY. I'll tell you everything, I promise. Just give me two minutes.

AARON. Or if you just wait there – ?

AARON *tries the door. Still stuck.*

Can you at least tell me your name?!

She's gone.

Hello?

Lights down on the corridor. The light of the moon throbs through the windowpane. AARON *looks at it. Eerie. Then – the door flies open – beep-beep! – All atmos out.* KATHERINE *there.*

Aaah! (*Seeing her.*) How did you open that door?

KATHERINE. There's a knack to it. Right, I'll show you where you'll be sleeping –

AARON. Did you see her?

KATHERINE. Her?

AARON. There was a woman. There. Talking to me.

KATHERINE. It can be quite noisy in the evenings. Now, if you follow me –

AARON *stands stock-still.*

Don't worry – the staff here live in luxury. They're treated just the same as the guests.

AARON. How?

KATHERINE. Whatever room is unoccupied on the night – you'll sleep in. So for you this evening that is… (*Checking tablet.*) Six-oh-four.

AARON *stares.*

(*Unimpressed.*) This way –

They move off. Lights down.

Lights up –

604

KATHERINE *and* AARON *standing in the exact same space.*

AARON. Oh. It really is… just the same. Is there a common room?

KATHERINE. A what?

AARON. A shared area?

KATHERINE. Oh no. You won't have to share anything. Total privacy. This is your buzzer –

KATHERINE *hands him one.*

Clever bit of technology. (*She swipes around on the iPad.*) It wakes you up for your shift –

She demonstrates – a unique alarm:

AUTOMATED VOICE. Scomodo Team Member – it is time to begin your shift.

KATHERINE. Then tells you when it's ending –

AUTOMATED VOICE. Your shift is now over – remember to charge your buzzer.

KATHERINE. When a room needs turning over –

Another sound.

– or if a guest rings for a room attendant –

An insistent buzz.

AARON. How long can I stay here?

KATHERINE. Well, tonight.

AARON. And then?

KATHERINE. Then you'll be assigned another room.

AARON. Every day?

KATHERINE. A change is as good as a rest. And you'll need your rest.

AARON. What about the other staff?

KATHERINE. No special treatment! They move rooms each night as well.

AARON. Do you know… if there's a girl who works here?

KATHERINE. There are several. Leave them alone. If you want to grab a name tag – ?

KATHERINE *holds out a box.*

AARON. Oh, I just – ?

AARON *looks through the box.*

(*Reading.*) Sandra… Jean-Philippe… Harmony… Derek… – Have you ever had an Aaron?

KATHERINE. Aaron? Why do you ask?

AARON. Well, just… because my name is Aaron.

KATHERINE. So it is. Very good. Look – you might as well take a few. They get lost easily.

AARON *grasps a big handful of name tags like pick-and-mix and pockets them. Noise bleeds in from the rooms above. Moving heavy cases, footsteps, chatter… Then something else is detectable… a woman's voice. Singing. Operatic. Beautiful. Just for a second.*

AARON. Sorry – can you hear that? Is that singing?

KATHERINE. There's a hen do on the floor below.

AARON. Not that kind of –

KATHERINE. Let's nip this in the bud. If I hear a word more about ghosts or any of that nonsense – I will put you on probation.

Bangs from an adjoining room.

Even light sleepers get used to the noise. Eventually.

AARON. That's a relief. I'm not a very good sleeper at all.

KATHERINE *shoots him a look.*

Not that that'll be a problem. (*Holding a cylinder of pills with a red band across.*) The doctor's given me some sleeping tablets. As a back-up. Just in c–

KATHERINE. Good, good. Well I'll leave you to settle in and get some rest before tomorrow. (*Reading off the iPad.*) On behalf of the Scomodo Hotel Group, I wish you a very warm welcome to the family.

Slam!

Door shut, KATHERINE *gone. Noise from the rooms around. Thumps. Moans. Talk radio.*

AARON *takes a drinking glass from the side, upturns it and listens to the floor. The noise intensifies. Drunkenness. Shouting. But no singing.*

He looks at the box of sleeping tablets. Opens them, takes one. Lights fade as noise of guests gets hazy until –

All at once noise out and lights up –

The beeper alarm is sounding.

AUTOMATED VOICE. Scomodo Team Member – it is time to begin your shift.

374

AARON *in a room with a* GLASWEGIAN GUEST *who looks a lot like* YOLANDA.

AARON. Oh, hello again! I didn't recognise you without your uniform. It's Yolanda, isn't it?

The GLASWEGIAN GUEST *looks blank.*

Oh. Are you not – ? Sorry, I could have sworn. I must be tired.

GLASWEGIAN GUEST. I told the girl to clean the room whilst I was out but she hasn't.

AARON. The… girl?

GLASWEGIAN GUEST. Aye. She said she'd clean it – but she can't have, 'cause the rat's still under the bed. (*Heading off*.) I've got a date – you deal with it.

AARON. The rat?!

GLASWEGIAN GUEST. Don't worry. I've roughed him up a bit. He's disorientated.

She disappears up the corridor.

Buzz – !

421

In the corridor, AMY *presses play on her Walkman.*
A YOUNGSTER *stares at her.*

YOUNGSTER. What *is* it?

AMY. It's a Walkman. For listening to music.

YOUNGSTER. You do know that you can listen to music on your phone?

AMY. I suppose I prefer stumbling across tapes at car-boot sales, in charity shops…

YOUNGSTER. Tapes?

AMY. They're giving them away! Especially this kind of music. I like very old music.

YOUNGSTER. Like Oasis and that?

AMY. A bit older. Look – (*Producing some tapes*.) last month I got *The Magic Flute*, *The Barber of Seville* and *Rigoletto* for twenty pee!

The YOUNGSTER *walks away, semi-disgusted…*

(*Desperately, chasing after her*.) Isn't that cool – ?!

Buzz – !

749

AARON *in the corridor – a* STRESSED GUEST *in the doorway of her room.*

STRESSED GUEST. The noise overnight was unbearable! Do you have any idea what it's like to be sleep-deprived?

AARON. Well I take these pills and they don't work – so yes. But – the noise – would you describe it as, say, lyrical? Where exactly did you hear it? Was it in a different language?

STRESSED GUEST. Don't walk rubbish! Lyrical? It was noise! I'm taking my business elsewhere. And I shall be lodging a complaint about you… (*Leaning and peering at his name badge.*) Derek.

Buzz – !

230

In the room – AMY *and a* WOMAN *with her hair in a towel, painting her nails.*

PAINTED NAILS. Crumpet needs his snack.

AMY. Crumpet?

Woof! A noise from a towel-covered box on the bed.

(*Tentatively.*) …You'd like *me* to – ?

PAINTED NAILS. Well obviously – ! I'm – (*Gesturing to her nails.*) His treats are just there.

AMY approaches the cage with a treat in hand –

AMY. How many do I – ?

PAINTED NAILS. One! Do they not train you here?

AMY. Not how to care for an –

PAINTED NAILS. Let me guess, it's your 'first day' as well?

AMY. As well?

PAINTED NAILS. As well as the other one.

AMY. Who?

PAINTED NAILS. The one who wouldn't shut up! Useless!
Took him an age to fix the lamp. I said it wasn't good enough
– he said he hadn't slept – ! The cheek – ! Making excuses…

AMY. He'd not slept?

PAINTED NAILS. Then he started gibbering on about –

AMY. Yes? About – ?

PAINTED NAILS. Oh, I can't remember. Opera or
something…

AMY (*animated, fast*). Opera?! It was him?! What did he say?
Was he asking after me? Had he figured it out – that she was
me? Singing? Is he coming back?

The WOMAN WITH PAINTED NAILS *turns slowly* –

PAINTED NAILS. You are all quite mad, here, aren't you?

AMY. But please, can you just tell me if –

PAINTED NAILS. Do not interrogate me in my own room!

Woof!

Hurry up, will you – he's starved!

AMY *approaches the cage* – Woof! *The dog bites her.*

AMY. Ouch!

PAINTED NAILS. And now you've frightened him!

Woof! Woof! Woof!

AMY (*begrudgingly*). I'm very sorry.

PAINTED NAILS. Leave him! I'll do it myself.

AMY *looks about the room. An idea* –

AMY. So he… fixed your lamp? My colleague?

PAINTED NAILS. You can go now.

The WOMAN *turns her attention entirely to her nails.*

AMY. Well I'll just… just double-check that it's working for you.

AMY approaches the lamp. She unscrews the bulb and places it on the floor. Then, takes her Walkman from her apron, and quietly places it on the floor alongside the bulb.

Right – yes – that's all fixed. He's done a great job, there.

The WOMAN WITH PAINTED NAILS *remains focused on her hands. The lights overhead flicker and a* GHOST *is visible for just a second, intrigued by what* AMY *is doing.*

(*Emphatically.*) But – you know – if you have any more problems with it – just call for a room attendant. Straight away. And one will come.

PAINTED NAILS. If you're hanging around for a tip, you're wasting your time.

Buzz – !

712

AARON *in the corridor with a* FRENCH COUPLE. *He looks tired.*

AARON. Did you call for a room attendant? Oh – is your door stuck? Here, they can be tricky –

He lets them in. There's a giant inflatable penis in the middle of the room. AARON *races to it and hides it behind his back just as the* COUPLE *turn around.*

And… (*Pointing desperately.*) Look! You've got a window! Seriously, go – have a look out of it! The view's amazing!

Bemused, the COUPLE *follow his pointing to the window –* AARON *stares at the penis, panics, then recalls his training with* MORAG. *He bites it. A pop! Which attracts the attention of the* COUPLE *as he quickly shoves it behind him, concealing it again.*

And you also have room attendants on call! (*Squeezing the air out of the inflatable as he talks to cover hissing.*) SO BASICALLY YOU CAN JUST CALL ANYTIME –

Hissssss –

EVERYONE LIVES ON SITE SO YOU CAN ALWAYS GET…

Hisssss –

HELP… (*Getting closer and closer to the ground as he gets the last of the air out.*) JUST CALL ON YOUR – (*Unable to reach or move, gesturing with his head instead.*) PHONE THERE – AND SOMEONE WILL COME.

Hissst. It's finally deflated. Now on the floor, from behind his back, he takes out the small resultant plastic mound and shoves it under his shirt.

(*Attempting nonchalance.*) So, do you have any questions…?

The COUPLE *look at each other.*

FRENCH PERSON 1. De quoi parle-t-il?

[What's he on about?]

FRENCH PERSON 2. Aucune idée.

[Not a clue.]

FRENCH PERSON 1. Mec, on ne parle pas très bien Anglais mais… on cherche le Science Museum – on est là?

[Mate, we don't speak English that well but… we're looking for the Science Museum – is this it?]

Buzz – !

108

Corridor. AMY *receiving an overflowing bin of beer cans from a* BUSINESSMAN *from his doorway. From his room, a radio advert blares: 'It's time. Time to show limescale who's boss.'*

AMY (*struggling*). What would Wagner say, eh? 'Ride of the Valkyries'. From carrying the bodies of fallen heroes over mountains to… advertising cleaning products!

BUSINESSMAN. What?

AMY. The music. It interests me. I'm thinking maybe I might be a singer one day.

The BUSINESSMAN *spits out his lager, laughing –*

BUSINESSMAN. They don't put cleaners on the telly! But if you want to be famous – there's always porn.

The slams his door in her face.

Buzz – !

230

In the room – WOMAN WITH PAINTED NAILS *and* AARON, *now very tired.*

PAINTED NAILS. Replace it! It's obviously faulty! Try it yourself –

AARON *attempts to switch it on and off – nothing. He crouches down and finds the bulb on the floor – strange. Then – he sees the Walkman. He picks it up.*

AARON. Does this belong to – ?

The lights overhead flicker.

PAINTED NAILS. What was that – ?

AARON. I uhm – I don't know…

AARON *looks at the Walkman – decides to keep it in his hand.*

PAINTED NAILS. This place is a joke.

AARON (*screwing the bulb back in*). Okay, that's working now. Is this yours, madam?

PAINTED NAILS. Eugh – of course not!

AARON. Right no. Absolutely. I'll leave you to settle in.

PAINTED NAILS (*low*). Whatever they pay you lot, it's too much…

End-of-shift alarm.

AUTOMATED VOICE. Your shift is now over – remember to charge your buzzer.

924

AARON *piles in through the door, knackered. He dumps his small bag.*

He goes to the bin and, from under his clothes, puts into it an L-plate on a string and the pancake of punctured penis. Various pairs of pants and other abandoned objects follow.

Then – the Walkman –

He looks at it, considers it – places it to one side.

Noises bleed in from the rooms above – arguments, sex, bangs of complaint on walls and floors as those awake awaken those sleeping. No song.

AARON *takes out his sleeping pills and takes a few.*

Lights down –

Lights up –

451

AMY *piles in through the door, knackered.*

Just as noisy here.

She goes to the bin and offloads pairs of pants and other abandoned objects. Noise from rooms around.

AMY *opens her suitcase. Full of cassette tapes. An ingenious set-up – a small deck with headphones that folds out. Ceremoniously, she selects a tape, puts it in and dons her headphones – a practised routine.*

Lights down –

Lights up –

924

AARON *is curled up as if in agony on his bed. He places his pillow over his ears. The rowdiness of guests intensifies. He looks up.*

AARON. When do you all *sleep*…?

The lights above him begin to flicker. AARON *takes out the sleeping tablets and swallows another one.*

He groans. Then sits bolt upright –

He paces the room. An idea –

The Walkman.

He places the headphones over his ears – and presses play. We hear what he hears.

At first the music melds with the sounds of madness from the guests above. Puccini. Then, plainly and clearly strings, and a tenor's voice.

TENOR'S VOICE.
Nessun dorma
Nessun dorma

[No one sleeps!
No one sleeps!]

Light and sound all at once. Everything changes.

AARON*'s eyes widen. The nature of reality bends – something indefinable sparkles. It reminds him of his first encounter in the hotel… At* AARON*'s window, behind him –* FIGARO *appears, invested in what is going on. The most intense swell of colour, light and sound.*

It's too much – !

AARON. Aaah!

AARON *presses stop –*

All in an instant – lights revert to normal, FIGARO *disappears and the noise of guests resurface.*

He holds the Walkman like it were a grenade with the pin taken out.

What the – ?

He stares at it.

The colour of blood… passion… And of the flames that engulfed those poor –

He gasps – realising that this must be a magical Walkman –

The work of the supernatural!

Still a little scared, he tentatively places the headphones back on his ears. He takes a deep breath and presses the play button.

FIGARO *reappears behind him.*

*Lights – lushness – * AARON *is utterly beguiled by the sound. He leans into it. Entranced.*

Music continues as –

Lights down –

Lights up –

451

AMY, *gazing out, her headphones on.*

TENOR'S VOICE.
Tu pure, o Principessa
Nella tua fredda stanza
Guardi le stelle
Che tremano d'amore e di speranza

[Even you, Princess
In your cold room
Watch the stars
Which tremble with love and hope]

A sequence as the music plays on –

Lights down –

[Day 3]

Lights up –

282

AARON *coming through the door, his shift ending. Marigolds on, holding a toilet brush, horror in his eyes.*

But there are precious tapes in his pockets.

TENOR'S VOICE.
> **Ma il mio mistero è chiuso in me**
>
> **[But my secret is sealed within me]**

Lights down –

[Day 9]

Lights up –

509

AMY *coming through the door, her shift ending. She yawns, takes out her stereo with a new tape – she sets about making another.*

TENOR'S VOICE.
> **Il nome mio nessun saprà**
>
> **[No one will know my name]**

Lights down –

Lights up –

631

AARON *coming through the door, his shift ending, unburdening himself from a record number of sex toys. Then – finally – another tape. He holds it up. Precious.*

TENOR'S VOICE.
> **No, no, sulla tua bocca lo dirò**
> **Quando la luce splenderà**
>
> **[I will reveal it only on your lips.**
> **When the daylight shines.]**

Lights down –

[Day 17]

Lights up –

114

AMY *coming through the door – she takes a glass and holds it to the floor – she listens.*

Lights down –

Lights up –

737

AARON *coming through the door, his shift ending.*

TENOR'S VOICE.
**Ed il mio bacio scioglierà il silenzio
Che ti fa mia**

**[And my kiss will break the silence
That makes you mine.]**

Lights down –

[Day 30]

Lights up –

278

AMY *can barely walk. She prises off her shoes. Her socks
are bloody. But she goes to make another tape.*

TENOR'S VOICE.
**Il nome suo nessun saprà.
E noi dovrem, ahimè, morir, morir.**

**[No one will know my name.
And we will have to die.]**

Lights down –

Lights up –

320

AARON *comes through the door, staggers to his bed, fully-
clothed. He takes a sleeping pill. And then a second. Then
a worrying handful. In his pocket – several new red cassette
tapes.*

*He kisses them – then takes out his full collection. He places
a new one carefully in the Walkman, places the headphones
on – climbs into bed –*

TENOR'S VOICE.
Dilegua, o notte
Tramontate, stelle
Tramontate, stelle
All'alba
Vincerò
Vincerò
Vincerò!

[Vanish, oh night.
Fade, you stars.
Fade, you stars.
At dawn
I shall win
I shall win
I shall win!]

Song concludes as AARON *reaches out one shaky hand to turn off his bedside lamp.*

He snores loudly.

Blackout as the music crescendos.

…

Alarm sound – !

Lights up –

813

AMY *in the corridor with a* MAN IN AN EYEMASK, *holding a pillow.*

EYEMASK. Is this down? Or feather? I was assured you used shredded memory foam pillows but this feels like down. I'll never get any sleep on this.

AMY. If you sent someone a love letter how long would you wait to hear back? A month?

EYEMASK. What?!

AMY. What about several love letters? Well – gifts. Special ones. From the depths of your soul that had taken you hours to carefully put together – ? And even if the person didn't know how to find you, they could leave a reply for you somewhere – couldn't they? Unless they were too shy? Could it be that?

EYEMASK. My pillow!

AMY. Sorry – I'll fetch you another. But… if I… forget – if it happened to slip my mind, maybe you could call for a room attendant again. (*A little desperately.*) And then if someone else turned up, you could give them a message from me? Or just keep them here a moment – lock them in the bathroom or something – ?

Buzz – !

199

AARON *enters the room. No one there. Some balloons – post-party. A large towel hung oddly off something.*

A note on the bed. He picks it up.

AARON (*reading*). Wife was sick on mattress. Sorry.

AARON *winces and lifts just the edge of duvet – yep. There it is.* AARON *puts on his red headphones, he takes out the most recent tape from his pocket and reads it.*

'*Car-men.*'

He puts it in the Walkman and presses play.

AARON *almost jumps out of his skin at the first bar of the overture – then – a fire in his eyes. It's incredible.*

Colour! Light from every available place! Wonder!

AARON *leaps for the balloons, popping them. He grabs the towel – his hips swinging out like a toreador – he performs suerte de capote.*

A sequence – perhaps in one room or over time in several. AARON *stands as if facing a bull – brandishing a toilet brush, triumphant – !*

CARMEN, *unmistakable, enters and lies on the bed seductively – flanked by two other* FACTORY WORKERS. *They wink at* AARON.

Doors fly open – two more TOREADORS *in full spectacular garb appear, behind and either side of* AARON *– all three perform a series of synchronised moves.*

He can imagine a crowd deafening him with their adulation. He bows. The room is magically clean.

Buzz – !

AARON *presses stop on his Walkman –*

All music, colour, sound, toreadors out at once in a snap-instant.

AARON *looks at his buzzer. Flashing and buzzing.*

I'm coming…

He quickly opens the Walkman to put the tape back in its case. But the tape gets caught and as he removes it, it tangles and twists in a stringy mess.

No! Oh – no no no!

Panicking, AARON *attempts to correct the situation. He places the Walkman down but keeps the tape in hand – then rushes to the desk to try and find a pencil for the tape. In his panic the tape is pulled long and then snaps! And as he whirls around on realising this – he accidentally treads on the Walkman.*

The crunch reverberates through his whole body.

He freezes. He can barely look.

He checks.

It's totally fucked.

He picks up the pathetic pieces of the machine in his hands. Irreparable. He can't contain his grief. The room feels beiger than ever. He looks about it. He is on the brink of despair.

Buzz – !

But has to go.

824
(Flickering a little/scrambled.)

AMY *with a* SOBER YOUNG WOMAN *in the corridor. The woman is wearing a negligee.*

AMY....a spider?

SOBER YOUNG WOMAN. I'm phobic. I can't go back in until it's been removed.

AMY. Are you… (*Looking her up and down.*) waiting for someone special?

SOBER. I shouldn't think that's any of your business! Could you hurry?

AMY. Sorry

She goes to enter. Then –

But – how did you know? If you were delusional or if it was… love?

SOBER. Is there something wrong with you?

AMY. Yes. That's what I'm thinking.

Buzz – !

724

AARON *in a dwam, fiddling with the hopeless bits of broken Walkman. There's a* MIDDLE-AGED COUPLE *in the room, the lights are flickering almost constantly –*

MIDDLE-AGED MAN. Can you imagine having to deal with that all day long?

MIDDLE-AGED WOMAN. It's driving us mad!

AARON *does nothing.*

MIDDLE-AGED MAN. Susan – did you book somewhere for dinner?

MIDDLE-AGED WOMAN. Jasper's gardener – what's he called? Toby. He recommended somewhere but I looked it up – it was all plastic seating and the waiters were wearing blue denim jeans. I don't know what he was thinking.

AARON. Do you believe in ghosts – ?

MIDDLE-AGED MAN. What?

AARON. Have you ever been to an opera – ?

MIDDLE-AGED WOMAN. Are you asking me out on a date – ?

MIDDLE-AGED MAN. Don't embarrass yourself, Susan –

MIDDLE-AGED WOMAN. Oh and be a darling a replace the duvet, will you? Richard spilling his wine. The slob.

AARON holds up the duvet – it looks Dionysian. A big red-wine stain.

AARON. Have you noticed things round here starting to feel… theatrical?

The posh pair frown at AARON, *utterly unsettled.*

MIDDLE-AGED MAN. What's he on about? Fix the lights, please!

AARON stares. The MAN *is frisking himself –*

My wallet, have you moved it?

MIDDLE-AGED WOMAN. Of course I've not moved it. And I don't know what you were suggesting about me and this young man –

MIDDLE-AGED MAN (*whilst looking around the room*). That you've flirted with every single 'young man' we've encountered – the train conductor, the taxi driver and now this… bellboy.

MIDDLE-AGED WOMAN. Men like it when I flirt with them! (*To* AARON.) Don't you?

MIDDLE-AGED MAN. It's gone. I can't believe it.

MIDDLE-AGED WOMAN. What?

MIDDLE-AGED MAN. This guy's stolen my wallet!

AARON. I haven't.

MIDDLE-AGED MAN. You think we'll put up with anything, don't you? Turn out your pockets.

MIDDLE-AGED WOMAN. Richard!

MIDDLE-AGED MAN (*aggressively*). Go on.

At a loss, AARON *does. From them he lays out all he has – the various smashed bits of Walkman, the unravelled red cassette tape, an old tissue and a pair of Y-fronts. The* MIDDLE-AGED MAN *is uncomfortable.*

MIDDLE-AGED WOMAN (*moving a cushion*). Here's your wallet, you cretin. (*She places a hand on* AARON*'s chest.*) Now are you going to apologise to my friend?

MIDDLE-AGED MAN. Don't be smug. I'm going out.

The MIDDLE-AGED MAN *throws on his hat.*

MIDDLE-AGED WOMAN (*unable to contain it*). Are you having an affair?

A couple of beats.

(*The room number flickers and dies.*)

MIDDLE-AGED MAN. What on earth makes you say that?

MIDDLE-AGED WOMAN. You've started wearing your hat at an angle.

MIDDLE-AGED MAN (*extremely defensive*). I wouldn't say that it was at an angle. (*To* AARON.) You wouldn't say this hat's at an angle, especially?

MIDDLE-AGED WOMAN. It's at an *absurd* angle, Richard. And you know it. It's positively… rakish, that angle. Your neck must be killing you just trying to balance it on there. What's her name?

MIDDLE-AGED MAN. I'm not talking to you if you're going to / be like this.

MIDDLE-AGED WOMAN. Look at the state of it! It's almost
    perpendicular!

MIDDLE-AGED MAN. You're mad – !

MIDDLE-AGED WOMAN. I imagine it'll fall off at any
    second – ! Go on, where did you meet her – ?

MIDDLE-AGED MAN. I'm not having a fucking affair!

His hat falls off.

Beat.

At the gym. I met her at the gym.

Very loud banging at the door. AARON *goes to open it –
a* DRUNK YOUNG WOMAN *runs in past him, flashing
her boobs.*

DRUNK YOUNG WOMAN. Haaaaaapppy birthdaaaaaaay!

Beat.

MIDDLE-AGED WOMAN. Is this her?

MIDDLE-AGED MAN. Strangely, no.

DRUNK YOUNG WOMAN (*lowering her top*). Is this the
    eighth floor?

AARON. Seventh.

DRUNK YOUNG WOMAN. Oh. Sorry! There's no number on
    the…

    Bye then!

She heads off –

Buzz – !

824
(*Flickering a little/scrambled.*)

SOBER YOUNG WOMAN *in a negligee in the corridor –*
AMY *emerges from the room with an upturned glass on
a piece of paper.*

SOBER (*to* AMY). Well – are you going to kill it?

AMY (*horrified*). No.

The DRUNK YOUNG WOMAN *comes careering down the corridor.*

DRUNK. There you are! I've been knocking on strangers' doors! I showed an old couple my tits! Happy birthday!

SOBER (*alarmed*). But – how did you know where I was?

DRUNK. You wrote it all down on the pad by your bed.

SOBER. You went into my bedr– ?

DRUNK. Yes! *Thank God!* Why would you want to spend your birthday on your own in a hotel like a weirdo? Now – here, take these in, will you, mate?

She shoves her carry-out into AMY*'s arms.* AMY *enters the room with them.*

I bought tins of gin and tonic – had a couple of those on the way here to pass the time but there's still plenty of –

SOBER. Look – you need to go.

DRUNK. What? Why?

SOBER. Because I'm seeing… my boyfriend.

DRUNK. You don't have a boyfriend.

SOBER. I do. I just haven't ever mentioned him.

DRUNK. Why?

SOBER. Because he's a bit… married.

DRUNK. *Oh my God? – WHAT?*

The DRUNK YOUNG WOMAN *screams.*

This is huge!

SOBER. Yes but stop shouting because he's staying here with his wife tonight –

DRUNK. In this room? That's *mental*!

SOBER. No, in a different room! But I just really wanted to see him on my birthday so I booked a room here too… and he's going to try and sneak out and see me – maybe – later, tonight – I don't know. When he can. But you can't tell *anyone*.

DRUNK. This is… Okay. I'm going.

SOBER. Wait! Do you have any Tampax?

DRUNK. Ehm… no.

SOBER. Shit!

DRUNK. On your period?

SOBER. I wasn't going to wear them as earrings.

DRUNK. Not got your keep cup?

SOBER. My what?

DRUNK. I mean, not – The other one? Menstrual cup!

SOBER. Yes… but I'm still getting used to it –

DRUNK. I know what you mean, there's a knack to it –

SOBER. Well, when I pulled it out just there it kind of… came out suddenly and –

The SOBER YOUNG WOMAN*, wincing, opens the door to the en suite, revealing a mad, dramatic-looking blood-spattered shower curtain. The* DRUNK YOUNG WOMAN *laughs.*

Shh! I'll have to clear it up before Richard gets here. (*To* AMY.) Can you get me a new shower curtain?

DRUNK. Richard? Is that his name? How old is he?

SOBER. Just – I'll tell you all about it later! Now bugger off!

DRUNK. Okay okay but before I go – *Haaaaapy birthday to youuuuuu!*

Another knock at the door. The DRUNK YOUNG WOMAN *answers. The* MAN IN AN EYEMASK *from earlier.*

EYEMASK. Excuse me, I'm trying to take a nap, could you please keep it down!

The MAN IN AN EYEMASK *gasps. He points to back wall of the en suite, horrified. The* SOBER YOUNG WOMAN *rushes to the en suite door and slams it shut. The* MAN IN AN EYEMASK *runs off up the corridor.*

Oh God – ! Aaaaaaaaaah!

DRUNK. It's alright, mate – I'm going! I'll be nice and quiet now! Apart from the sound of –

The DRUNK YOUNG WOMAN *mimes having sex in an attempt to make her sober friend laugh, yelling 'Oh Richard!' as she wanders up the corridor.*

Buzz – !

(*Numbers scrambled.*)

AARON *in the corridor. The* MAN IN AN EYEMASK *races past him.*

EYEMASK. There's been a murder in our midst! At first –
I heard screaming! Then the next thing – blood all over their shower curtain! (*Paranoid.*) They got too good a look at me… They know I know. I can't stay here – it's every man for himself! I'm making a run for it – !

724
(*Flickering a little/scrambled.*)

The MIDDLE-AGED WOMAN *who is throwing her husband's belongings into the bin, unaware of* AMY.

MIDDLE-AGED WOMAN. You won't be needing your cufflinks, your Rolex, your stupid shitty books that you bang on about –

AMY. Can I help you, madam?

MIDDLE-AGED WOMAN. Bring me a bottle-opener, will you?

AMY. That's not something we provide, I'm afraid.

MIDDLE-AGED WOMAN. What kind of hotel is this? The young lad couldn't fix the lights – you can't even bring me a bottle-opener. You're all incompetent. Do you know him – the other one? He seems mad?

AMY. Um… no. I'm not sure that I do know him. I thought, at one point that maybe I did. But… I suppose *that* was mad because… we haven't actually, properly, met.

MIDDLE-AGED WOMAN. Keep it that way. (*Spiteful.*) You know they're all the same, don't you?

Men.

(*Holding the bin out.*) Empty this for me?

They don't care about us. All our efforts? They mean nothing to men. They might seem interested at first but then they forget us in an instant. If you believe anything else, darling – you're kidding yourself.

The evidence will surface. You find the proof eventually – that they couldn't care less.

AMY. Well… I don't know. I've been looking for proof that he does care. But proof that he doesn't… What would that even –

AMY looks into the bin. She picks out the contents.
A destroyed tape. All the smashed pieces of the red Walkman.

No…?

She exits hurriedly to the corridor, clutching the pieces.
She sinks to the floor to one side of a huge trolley of sheets.
Staring at the mess.

Did it not mean… anything?

Her buzzer goes. She takes it off and throws it against the wall.

AARON *enters the corridor and approaches the door –*
unaware of AMY.

The hotel is noisy. There is something indistinct amongst the cacophony. Both lovers stop to listen a moment – sensing something but…

The MIDDLE-AGED WOMAN *emerges from the hotel-room door and grabs* AARON, *pulling him into the darkness of the room.*

AMY *senses something – stands – wipes tears from her eyes to look. But no. There's no one there.*

She picks up her discarded buzzer and exits.

The MIDDLE-AGED WOMAN *in her room. She is drinking red wine from the bottle.* AARON *stands awkwardly alongside.*

MIDDLE-AGED WOMAN. Have a drink with me.

He looks at his shoes.

You married?

He shakes his head.

Good. That's the start that marks the end. The beginning of all the… disappointment.

It's not that he was sleeping with another woman…

It's that he looked me in the eye every day whilst he was.

Came in her bed. Farted in mine.

And you've got to remember – I was handing him the shirts – I was *handing them to him*… the nice, crisp, clean, ironed shirts…

I was buying the aftershave…

I was facilitating that affair. I preserved him. Stopped him from rotting. (*Drinking heavily.*)

AARON *picks up the phone*

AARON. Is there someone I could call?

MIDDLE-AGED WOMAN. Phone's gone dead.

AARON *listens. It's true. He looks at his buzzer – nothing.*

AARON. Something's not working…

MIDDLE-AGED WOMAN (*anger turning to sorrow*). And I haven't slept in bloody weeks because I was so sure something was going on. Too scared to ask. Easier to argue about anything else.

And now that I know for sure, he's finally said it and finally buggered off – can I sleep…?

Can I fuck.

She starts to move towards the window.

AARON. Madam?

She opens it and tries to force it wider, but there is a safety catch.

MIDDLE-AGED WOMAN. No… Don't come near me!

AARON. What are you doing?

MIDDLE-AGED WOMAN. Look – I'm wide awake. I'm not going to slip or anything.

Noises start to bleed in from other rooms. Sex.

Do you hear that?! That's him!

AARON. It's always noisy in here. It could be anyone.

MIDDLE-AGED WOMAN. I know that sound. That's him and her!

She pulls at the window. It doesn't open far.

What's this?

AARON. It's a safety catch.

MIDDLE-AGED WOMAN. But we need some fresh air in here!

She kicks it a few times –

AARON. That'll set off an alarm.

MIDDLE-AGED WOMAN. Good! Something to drown out the sound of them!

It buckles. The window swings unnaturally wide open.

Where's the alarm? You promised me an alarm!

AARON. The whole system must be down –

MIDDLE-AGED WOMAN. I can still hear them!

AARON. Can I… hold your hand?

MIDDLE-AGED WOMAN. Don't touch me! You're not allowed to! Stay away!

AARON. Shall we have that drink?

MIDDLE-AGED WOMAN. Sure, he's a bastard… but I'm no better because I can tell that I'm going to miss the bastard.

AARON. Please?

MIDDLE-AGED WOMAN. I just want to feel what it's like for a moment –

Noise from the other room. 'Oh! Richard!'

The pair of… shits!

She climbs onto the windowsill. AARON *approaches her.*

If you come any closer I will fucking jump – !

He freezes, petrified.

Don't look at me like that! I'm joking. You can take a joke?

AARON *looks about desperately.*

I don't want to… Not like this. I just want to sleep!

The noises from the adjoining rooms get worse. Banging of headboards – cries of ecstasy – AARON *knows he has to do something. He clears his throat. It's a bit shaky at first. Donizetti. (Surtitles optional for this section.)*

I'm sorry. I'm so sorry to do this to you, but I just can't listen to it any more, *I can't* – !

AARON *(a cappella).*
Una…
furtiva lagrima
negli occhi suoi spuntò:

[A…
furtive tear
in her eyes appeared:]

She turns and stares at him.

**Quelle festose giovani
invidiar sembrò**

[She seemed to envy those young festive girls]

An accompaniment is gently present now. The sounds of other guests all about fade.

**Che più cercando io vo?
Che più cercando io vo?**

**[What more is there to prize?
What more is there to prize?]**

She turns from the window and walks safely back into the middle of the room, captivated.

**M'ama! Sì, m'ama,
Lo vedo, lo vedo.**

**[She loves me! Yes, she loves me,
I see it. I see it.]**

The song concludes.

MIDDLE-AGED WOMAN. That was…

They look at each other. He is as surprised as her.

Where did you learn to do that?

AARON. I don't know.

AARON *helps her into her bed. He closes the window.*

Is there anything I can get you?

MIDDLE-AGED WOMAN. Would you… just a bit more?

He prepares himself, forms the shape with his mouth, takes a breath but –

She lets out a huge snore. Passed out.

AARON *looks at her. Switches off her lamp.*

He exits to the corridor, in shock. He paces.

AARON. What does this mean?!

He addresses the walls – unsure where to send his message.

What are you trying to tell me? Ghost… Singer-spirit-god? Whatever-you-are?

No response.

Is that why you left me the red tapes?

Nothing.

Do you even speak English? I'm sorry if I'm not doing this right?

Nothing.

He has an idea –

Saint-Saëns. A capella at first.

Mon cœur s'ouvre à ta voix…

[My heart opens to your voice…]

He thinks. He knows it all.

Mon cœur s'ouvre à ta voix…

[My heart opens to your voice…]

A GHOST OF THE OPERA *appears, very interested in this…*

Comme s'ouvrent les fleurs
Aux baisers de l'aurore

[Like the flowers open
To the kisses of the dawn]

A beat.

929

AMY, *alone in her room. Suitcase alongside – closed. Head in her hands. She doesn't listen to any music.*

Then – suddenly – she looks up. She can hear something.

She races to grab a glass, upturns it and places it on the floor –

AARON.
> **Mon cœur s'ouvre à ta voix**
> **Comme s'ouvrent les fleurs**
> **Aux baisers de l'aurore**
>
> **[My heart opens to your voice**
> **Like the flowers open**
> **To the kisses of the dawn]**

She gasps.

She knows.

He heard it all.

Her eyes well up.

She takes a breath and responds –

AMY.
> **Mais, ô mon bienaimé,**
> **Pour mieux sécher mes pleurs,**
> **Que ta voix parle encore!**
>
> **[But, oh my beloved,**
> **To better dry my tears,**
> **Let your voice speak again!]**

Lights up on AARON *in the corridor.*

They duet.

Everything changes – the space is light-filled and beautiful – a full orchestra magically accompanies them.

BOTH.
> **Ah! Réponds, réponds à ma tendresse!**
>
> **[Ah! Respond, respond to my tenderness!]**

Several GHOSTS *appearing now – extremely invested. Finally two young lovers are singing together – there is enormous potential here.*

> **Verse-moi, verse-moi l'ivresse!**
> **Rréponds à ma tendresse**

Réponds à ma tendresse!
Ah! Verse-moi, verse-moi l'ivresse!

[Make me drunk with ecstasy!
Respond to my tenderness
Respond to my tenderness!
Ah, make me, make me drunk with ecstasy!]

Bang – ! Sparks fly overhead. The lights flicker.

AMY*, breathless in her room.* AARON *likewise in a corridor.*

Music in more fully than ever – the play has become an opera. Everything is music now. The beginning of a new song –

AARON. That girl! She's the only one with the answers! She knows how to find the ghosts – she knows why they found me! I have to see her!

Lights down on the corridor as AARON *dashes off.* AMY *still visible in her room –*

AMY. You were listening!
    …I have to see you.
    What's nine hundred doors…?
    When I know you're behind one of them.

Energised, she leaps to her feet and out of her room –

(*All the following sung would also be surtitled for the audience.*)

Lights up in the hallway – light fixtures hang low from the ceiling. The place is falling to pieces, literally.

?

AMY *knocking urgently on a door –*

AMY.
    Housekeeping!

HALF-ASLEEP GUEST.
    I'm sleeping!

AMY.

Well, I'm coming in –

HALF-ASLEEP GUEST (*emerging from his room, to the corridor*). You mustn't – I've not got my eight hours in.
Before, you were nowhere to be seen!
This noise is insane and my room needs a clean!
The screens have stopped working – there's widespread confusion!
And every five minutes, another intrusion.

AMY.

/ But –

HALF-ASLEEP GUEST.

The thermostat is broken, I can't use the phone
No one can tell if their room is their own
Are all of the staff here just constantly shirking?

AMY.

No, sir, it's these buzzers, they're no longer working.
So, no one can call us – but now that I'm here –

HALF-ASLEEP GUEST.

You can close my door again and dis-ap-pear.

AMY.

You don't understand, you see this is an emergen/cy.

HALF-ASLEEP GUEST.

If only you'd hoover my room with similar urgency…

Declarative –

AMY.

I seek a man. Works here. He's an –

HALF-ASLEEP GUEST.

'*Odd ball*'
I know, I just heard all of this through the wall!
You just asked my neighbours, I got it verbatim.
To hear it again causes novel frustration for
Ev'ry word of this I've just discerned!

AMY.
>I can't take the risk of a stone left unturned.
>You seen him?

HALF-ASLEEP GUEST.
>No –

AMY.
>Well if you do / pass this on!

HALF-ASLEEP GUEST.
>Pass this on… I know!

AMY.
>Since it looks like our room numbers have gone
>We need to meet somewhere that cannot be mistaken
>That is, if his feelings, like mine, are unshaken.
>This is my plan – and I think it's foolproof
>We climb all the stairs –

HALF-ASLEEP GUEST.
>'And meet on the roof.'
>*I know.* That's twice your full speech has been heard –

>*She moves off –*

AMY.
>Must go one door down –

HALF-ASLEEP GUEST.
>And treat me to a third?!

AMY.
>I'll change it – I'll make it sound quite off-the-cuff!

HALF-ASLEEP GUEST.
>Get out of my sight now!

AMY.
>Alright. Fair enough.

>*She exits up the corridor.*

>*Lights down –*

?

A TOURIST *and* AARON, *enthused by a potential solution, in the corridor –*

AARON.

Oh, I know – I'll stay here and then you can call!
Like you need something… – ach like – anything at all!
She'll heed it and come here and then she'll be found!
Wait – !
The whole system's down so the buzzers won't sound!
If only I knew what she looked like – her name!
Oh what can we do?

TOURIST.

Mate, you're clearly insane.

Lights down –

Lights up in the room –

?

Two LADS *in sombreros and flip-flops, passed out, empty tequila bottles in hand.*

AMY (*prodding them*).

Sit up please and listen, you two – come along!
He must know the plan. We can't get this wrong!

Lights down –

Lights up on the corridor –

?

A WOMAN IN A TOWEL –

AARON.

Please help me – I need you, I must solve this mystery –
She works here, she gets it – knows all of the history – !

TOWEL.

Never mind that – get my shower fixed first!

AARON.

You could have a sink wash, if worse comes to worst?

TOWEL.
How dare you!

AARON.
I'm sorry – I'm just in a rush! There's a girl I must find who knows how to get –

TOWEL.
Shush!
I don't make complaints and I'm rarely dramatic
But those waterworks are completely erratic!

A MOTHER WITH BABY *bursts in –*

MOTHER.
Young man I insist on this woman's removal!
The racket – !

TOWEL.
And why do I need your approval?!

MOTHER.
You did all this yelping, my son couldn't sleep –

TOWEL.
The cause was a wild fluctuation of heat –

MOTHER.
But now my poor little boy will not drop off!

TOWEL.
But my shower – it went hot, cold, hot, cold, cold, off!

MOTHER.
So that was cause, was it? Just a cold shower?
You liar – your screaming went on for an hour.

TOWEL.
Well if anything in here worked nearly at all,
You wouldn't have heard a damn thing through that wall!

MOTHER.
It can't just have been that – the sound was so strange –
The noises you made were completely deranged!

TOWEL.

Go on then – recall them! Do us an impression!

MOTHER.

They had more or less *this* harmonic progression –
(*Virtuoso.*) Ooooohh –
Eeee – ha-hoooh…
Ohh – oh – oh – oh – Aaaaaah!
Oh-ho ha hee hah – oooooooh – !
Ha
Ho
Heeee – hwoooooooooaaah
Hah-hee-hoh-eeee-oh-ooaaaaaeeeeee-AAAAAAAAAAA A
OOOOOOOOHHHHHHHHHHH!

(*Interrupting herself.*) Actually – if it were ice-cold intense…
That would explain – sorry, makes perfect sense.

Lights down –

?

A COUPLE *right in the middle of having sex, frozen in shock.*

AMY.

Just to be certain, I'll ask you once more,
You don't think you've seen him? Both totally sure?
He'd be asking strange questions all of the time –
And wearing a uniform sim'lar to mine?

Beat.

No?

Lights down –

Lights up –

?

AARON *knocks on a room door,* HALF-ASLEEP GUEST *appears, stepping into the corridor*

AARON.

I hope you can help, sir!

HALF-ASLEEP GUEST.
God, what fresh hell…

AARON.
I'm conducting a search of this mad hotel!

HALF-ASLEEP GUEST.
Now I wouldn't say that I'm all that demanding
But it begs belief that this place is still standing

AARON.
I hear you, I'll log it – I just need a word –

HALF-ASLEEP GUEST.
No! *This* is my feedback and *it will be heard*!
What kind of dump is this? The mess! The disgrace!

AARON.
Like a… magical, horrible, wonderful place?
Now I know my concerns may sound smaller and sillier

HALF-ASLEEP GUEST.
Hold on… your expression, it seems so… familiar?
Oh no – don't tell me – you are, you're In Love!
She was here. There's a plan. She waits. Up above

AARON.
– Hold on –

A change.

…Love?

HALF-ASLEEP GUEST.
Oh, come on don't give me that look.
You *must* know you are! Get a clue! It's textbook.
You've dilated pupils, you're shaking and sweating
The adrenalin flooding your brain needs offsetting
A force like no other's enraptured your soul
You're nervous, obsessive, you've lost all control!
You're high as a kite! And all sense has gone from you!
Why, what did *you* think it was that was wrong with you?

AARON (*processing*).
Well weeks ago, sir, I witnessed a sight

That filled me at once with joy, wonder and fright
A woman – singing – it changed my whole world
Since then, so much unfettered beauty has unfurled!
Her voice brought about in me such excitation
I knew there could only be one explanation

HALF-ASLEEP GUEST.
You'd met the one person you needed the most?

AARON.
Well no – I assumed… what I'd seen was a ghost.

Beat.

The HALF-ASLEEP GUEST *looks at him.*

Then I met someone else, but through a partition
Who took away my every last inhibition
She got a truth out of me no one else could
And for once in my whole life – I felt understood.
And then when I told her about what I'd seen
She didn't seem shocked at all –

HALF-ASLEEP GUEST.
Jesus, you're green.

AARON.
She knew all about opera too, when I mentioned.

HALF-ASLEEP GUEST.
And all of this time –

AARON.
I'd not made the connection!
I said I must refind the ghost, hear it sing
And she said –

HALF-ASLEEP GUEST.
'As it goes, I could pull a few strings'

AARON.
Then I found a lost Walkman which seemed unconventional –

HALF-ASLEEP GUEST.
And you didn't think 'losing' it might be intentional?

AARON.
Oh God! That was her – I'm so stupid and lame.

HALF-ASLEEP GUEST.
She is your ghostie. They're one and the same.

AARON.
But my whole world transformed –

HALF-ASLEEP GUEST.
'Cause you've got all the feels!
That's what it's like when you're head over heels

AARON.
I hear strings, I see colour – wherever I go.

HALF-ASLEEP GUEST.
That's true love alright
Look at you, you're aglow.
The way you described that first conversation
It moved me, I must say
I felt your elation

AARON.
I addoooooooooored her

HALF-ASLEEP GUEST.
You adoooooooooooored her

AARON.
From the very first moment I saaaaw her
Then I adooooooooooored her
For a second time, but through a dooooooooooooor, sir.

HALF-ASLEEP GUEST.
Now get it together – She's up on the roof.
And she's desperate to see you, to tell you the truth.

Several beats.

AARON.
No?!

Beat. AARON *can't believe it.*

You seem like a trustworthy kind of a bloke
But my heart couldn't take it if this was a joke
I need just to know I've no reason to doubt you.

HALF-ASLEEP GUEST.
    I'm sure she's your girl. She knew things about you.

AARON.
    Like what?

HALF-ASLEEP GUEST.
    That you're strange. A right pain in the arse.

AARON.
    Did she give you a name?

HALF-ASLEEP GUEST.
    No, the details were sparse, but she's some set of pipes!

AARON.
    Must be her – !

HALF-ASLEEP GUEST.
    She can sing. More than that – she can belt it.
    Wee talented thing.

AARON.
    This is it…
    Yes, it's true…
    All of this…
    All of this…
    All of this…
    Was you?

    (*To the* HALF-ASLEEP GUEST.) Should I go up there now?

HALF-ASLEEP GUEST.
    No – I'd wait till next week.

AARON.
    You're funny! I love you!

HALF-ASLEEP GUEST.
    Oh fuck off! Let me sleep!

AARON *sprints up the corridor as the* GUEST *disappears back into his room –*

Lights down –

Music changes, Tchaikovsky. Letter scene, Eugene Onegin.

An new aperture opens above the set.

Slowly, above the room and corridor, is revealed a beautiful, detailed Victorian roof space. The crowning glory of The Grand Old Opera House.

There is a single door leading onto it –

Through it, AMY *enters.*

Above her – the night sky.

She looks around. No one. She paces.

She sings.

AMY.
Быть может, это все пустое,
Обман неопытной души,
И суждено совсем иное?…

[Perhaps this is all meaningless
The delusions of a naive soul
Perhaps fate holds something altogether different for
me?…]

Lights down –

Lights up on the corridor below –

?

AARON *there running, breathless, trying to get to the roof when a* MAN, *massaging his bad neck, enters furious. Music changes – Rossini, 'Largo al Factotum'.*

BAD NECK.
Finally – ! A member of staff!
Hoooow can I *sleep* with a *crick* in my *neck like* this?
See it *hurts* when I *turn* to the *left –* (*Demonstrating.*) Aaah!

Hooooow can a man *sleep* with a *crick* in his *neck like this*?
I won't *rest* till the *mat*ter's add*ressed*.

AARON *tries to duck past him – the* MAN *corners him –*

I'm clienteeeeeeeeelé
In a hote-l-é
In a hote-l-é
Of quality!
Of quality!

AARON.
Don't look at me. Somewhere to be!

Music transitions – Mozart, La Nozze di Figaro *overture.*

A TEMPESTUOUS WOMAN *corners* AARON –

TEMPESTUOUS.
Lights have bloody *blown.*
Tried the bloody *phone* but there's no *bloody* dial *tone*!
How's a woman s*posed* to make this *known* without a *blood*y
mega*phone* – I should have *bloody* stayed at *home.*

'Scuse me, dear?

AARON.
Not now I –

TEMPESTOUS.
D'yu work here?

AARON.
Well yes but –

TEMPESTUOUS (*suddenly insane with rage*).
WEEEE'VE SPENT
A FOR-*TUNE* ON THIS TRIP *THE* ROOM WE'VE
GOT'S.
A.
BLOO–
–DY.
TIP!

AARON.
Very sorry madam and I'm

Very sorry sir
Whilst I want to help you and I'm hearing your concerns
You're going to need to wait for my return.

AARON *makes a run for it – the* TEMPESTUOUS
WOMAN *grabs him.*

Aaah!

TEMPESTUOUS (*pushing herself forward*).
I am first!

BAD NECK.
This is worse!

TEMPESTUOUS (*turning on* BAD NECK).
BO-LLOCKS!
With all *that* we've been through *you* know I
Have.
A.
Mind.
To.
SUE!

Lights down –

Lights up –

The roof. AMY *is restless, waiting.*

AMY.
Вообрази: я здесь одна!
Никто меня не понимает!

[Imagine, here I am. Alone!
No one understands me!]

The corridor. 'Libiamo' – La Traviata *– waltz time –*
a FASCINATOR WOMAN *appears, plummy, dressed for*
a formal occasion. She pins AARON *to the wall –*

FASCINATOR.
Uh, *paaaa*rdon me *room* three-oh-*three* sprang a *leeeeeaaaak*
Which then *dripped* on my sister's *dress*
Which was in the *trou*ser press

(We've a –)
Christening tomorrow – and whilst I am suited,
She's *got* not a stitch to *wear* –
and electro*cu*ted.

AARON.
I can't / help –

TEMPESTOUS (*pushing in front*).
Whilst this lady's leak is reg*re*ttable
She could simply *take* a re*cep*tacle
And *place* it be*neath* where the *drips* come down
Just un*til* they can *send* someone *round*.

AARON.
Can I go now / please – ?!

FASCINATOR.
(So)
Roooom three-oh-*three* damna*bly* satur*aaaaates*?
What whilst *I*, and my sister *bliiiithe*ly, cele*brate*?

BAD NECK.
Aaaah! What whilst *she*, and her sister *blithe*ly, cele*brate*?

TEMPESTUOUS.
Oh for goodness' sake!

Lights down –

Lights up –

The roof.

AMY (*distressed*).
Рассудок мой изнемогает,
И молча гибнуть я должна!
Я жду тебя,
Я жду тебя!

[I'm going mad
Will I perish here in silence?
I wait for you!
I wait for you!]

Lights down –

Lights up –

The corridor.

Music transitions, La Nozze di Figaro *overture, fast strings –*

A WOMAN ON A HEN DO *enters, startled by the commotion. She wears deely boppers and other daft hen do paraphernalia.*

The MAN WITH BAD NECK *blocks* AARON*'s exit entirely. He is now surrounded by five irate customers.*

HEN.
 Whoa –
 What's the fuss?

BAD NECK/FASCINATOR/TEMPESTUOUS (*to* AARON).
 *An*swer us!

AARON.
 There isn't / time – !

FASCINATOR.
 USE-LESS! This place is just dilapidated –

BAD NECK.
 And it's poorly ventilated –

BAD NECK/FASCINATOR.
 How will we be compensated?

FASCINATOR.
 My dear sister's devastated!

HEN.
 Wow youse all are agitated

FASCINATOR.
 Sssh, you are inebriated!

HEN.
 This has really escalated

BAD NECK/FASCINATOR.
 We must be remunerated!

FASCINATOR.

It cannot be overstated!

HEN.

Aye – as you've all demonstrated…

Music changes. Drums. Then melody in – slower, calmer, the tune of Wagner's 'Treulich geführt'.

Sorry, me a-*gain*
Here on a *hen.*
Hate tae interrupt yous
But's *embdy* goat a *pen*?

(We)
*Wa*ntae play the *game*
(*Sticking a blank Post-it to her forehead.*)
Where *obdy* hus a *name* (could have)
Sworn I packed a *bi*ro (but it)
Must be back at *hame.*

Now what has got youse angry?
(*Indicating* AARON.) Is he the one to blame?

Music transitions – Offenbach, Orpheus in the Underworld *'Can Can'.*

WOMAN ON A HEN DO *exits. Strings – pulsing – building…*

FASCINATOR.

Well the…
*Fir*st thing *was*, our *ke*ttle *blew*
We *cou*ldn't *ev*en *make* a *brew*
The *milk* had turned a *gr*eenish-*blue*

BAD NECK.

The *bis*cuits *taste* like bloody *glue*!

FASCINATOR.

The *lit*tle *chair* did *look* brand *new*
But *I* could *see* a *loo*sened *screw*
It *caught* my *ja*cket, *tore* right *through*

BAD NECK.
My *car*pet *needs* at*ten*ding *to!*

AARON.
Please slow down sir,
And you, madam, you're too fast
Might I offer that these issues are all classed
In the or-der of their seniority
To afford a sense of the priorities –

Accompaniment returns – building into can-can section… it
surges and –

AARON.	FASCINATOR/
And then I'll come	TEMPESTUOUS
And sort it out	(*nodding*).
But now just let me	Uh-huh
Go just let me	Uh-huh
Go just let me	Uh-huh
Go just let me	Uh-huh
Go	Uh-huh
Go	Uh-huh
Go	/ Uh-huuhhhh.
Go	
Go	
Go	

BUSYBODY.
'Scuse me – !
Something's blocking up my toilet
Nothing will dislodge it
And no one has come to take a look but also –

It's so creepy in this hotel, there's a funny damp smell
And I had a tepid bath as well.

FASCINATOR/TEMPESTUOUS.
Something's blocking up her toilet!
Nothing will dislodge it!
And no one had come to take a look but also –

It's so creepy in this hotel, there's a funny damp smell
And she had a tepid bath as well!

Transition into final section – all voices start to layer. The
MAN WITH BAD NECK *and* WOMAN ON A HEN DO
doing indistinct wailing whist the others continue to complain.

BUSYBODY.	AARON.	TEMP.	FASC.
Something's blocking up my toilet	I'm sorry, *miss –*	Sheets all crumpled!	First thing was, the kettle blew
		We're disgruntled!	We couldn't even make a brew
Nothing will dislodge it	I didn't *know –*	Much perturbance!	The milk had turned a greenish-blue
And no one has come to take a look but also –	I cannot stay –	Noise disturbance!	
	Please let me go!	En suite grimy!	It made my husband want to spew
It's so creepy in this hotel, there's a funny damp smell	I have no choice –	Windows tiny!	The little chair did look brand new
		You want slapping!	
And I had a tepid bath as well.	If you kick off –	And then sacking!	But I could see a loosened screw
	I'll have to run –		It caught my jacket, tore right through (what)
	Oh just fuck off! Fuck! Off!		Are you going to do?!

The lights flicker in the hallway – then cut out!

Darkness.

Commotion and disorientation. Lights back up –

The guests are all in the corridor but AARON *is gone.*

FASCINATOR. Where is he?

TEMPESTUOUS. He's run away! The little – !

BUSYBODY. Did anyone get a look at his name badge?

FACINATOR. I think it said… Jean-Phillipe.

Lights down –

Lights up on the roof –

?

AMY *backs towards the door, giving up hope.*

She sings a single, vulnerable note.

Then –

*Wham! All music out as the door behind her flies open,
knocking her out and concealing her –*

A WORKER IN A HARD HAT *enters, entirely unawares,*
KATHERINE *alongside.*

HARD HAT. Now please be *very careful*. We're at height –
there can be all kinds of unexpected hazards. And that is…
(*Checking his clipboard.*) yes, yet another door with
a misaligned strike plate which could lead to sticking –

At that moment, AARON *runs through the fire door –
sweating, breathless – awaiting the single most important
moment of his life.*

KATHERINE. Aaron? Staff training's one floor down. You can
wait for me there –

AARON. Katherine! It's you! But where's she – is she not here
yet?

MORAG *appears at the open door –*

MORAG. Staff training?

KATHERINE. It's on floor nine, Morag. I'm just getting the
results of our building assessment.

MORAG *goes to leave –*

HARD HAT. But leave that open, please! It's poorly installed and we'll need access back to the fire escape.

AARON. Morag!

MORAG. You alright?

AARON. And are you, *you*?

MORAG. Ehm, aye, I think so.

KATHERINE. If you two don't mind – I am in a meeting – !

Beat.

AARON. Wait –

A couple of beats.

Where's the music?

AARON looks about him as if he might see it –

MORAG. Are you alright?

AARON. It's so quiet. Why isn't there any music?

KATHERINE. Music? We're on the roof.

AARON. But you all saw the things that happened?

KATHERINE. I think we're well aware of the infrastructural issues! That is the whole purpose of this assessment, if you could stop interrupting. (*To* HARD HAT.) Now, in terms of the building's other… idiosyncrasies – what duties do the staff need to perform?

MORAG. An exorcism?

HARD HAT. Well, I imagine doors have been slamming?

MORAG. Aye, some of them are poltergeists.

HARD HAT. Lights flickering? Short-circuiting?

MORAG. There's so much unrest here. Heartbroken lovers, you see, separated by a wall of fire.

HARD HAT. Okay, I don't know what that means exactly but –
the en suite extractors will need cleaning and, in some cases,
replacing. Also – when did you last conduct a fire drill?

KATHERINE. It can't have been that –

MORAG. Never.

HARD HAT. We must conduct a fire drill *today*. Test your alarm,
remind everyone of the meeting point and the protocol.

KATHERINE. Of course. We can do that. Morag – ! Wait
downstairs. Tell the others we'll begin training with a fire drill.

MORAG. Aye, aye, in a minute – but, Katherine, look at the
view from up here! I'd never have guessed – it's that
beautiful!

HARD HAT (*looking at his list*). I'm afraid there's also
evidence of someone smoking in the rooms –

MORAG. Beautiful-schmootiful, I'll go and do as you say,
Katherine, let everyone know about this drill. Very
important.

MORAG *goes*.

AARON. No, Morag, don't go – tell them the story! About the
opera house!

HARD HAT. Besides this, your linens aren't fire retardant,
we've found traces of hazardous chemicals in the tap water –

GENERIC STAFF MEMBER *appears*.

AARON. Mohammed! Help me –

GENERIC STAFF MEMBER. It's Sarah.

AARON. Sarah! Right yes – Sarah – You'll know where she is?
The other one who works here – have you seen her?

GENERIC STAFF MEMBER. Who?

KATHERINE. Training is on floor nine! I'm receiving the
building assessment –

GENERIC STAFF MEMBER. Oh finally, so – have we got ghosts?

HARD HAT. No… you've got faulty extractors. It's caused a build-up of condensation which has worked its way into the electrics in most of the building. This is badly affecting your lights.

GENERIC STAFF MEMBER.…Is that it?

HARD HAT. It's also resulting in sudden downdraughts, which is what's causing the doors to slam.

GENERIC STAFF MEMBER. I feel a bit daft, now… Oh, well. You live and learn.

GENERIC STAFF MEMBER *exits*.

AARON. Hold on –

YOLANDA *appears* –

YOLANDA. Staff training?

KATHERINE. When I said 'top floor' I meant the top internal floor of the building! Not the highest you can possibly go! If we could all just employ a bit of common sense in this place – it would save me a lot of time. Ask yourselves – are we *likely* to be conducting training on the roof? No! What's an alternative explanation, then? Are we *likely* to work in a building haunted by ghosts – ?

AARON (*raising his voice*). Yes!

They look at AARON.

Or I don't know but I don't… I don't buy all this.

HARD HAT. Well it's here in black and white –

AARON. Not that, I'm sure that's all true but there *is* something else going on. There has to be. Come on! There was… (*Getting tearful.*) There was *music*. You must have heard it? Yolanda?

Beat. They look at AARON *a little pitifully.*

Why are you looking at me like that? There was music all
through this place! And I was part of it! I made this beautiful
sound!

YOLANDA. Maybe you need some sleep – ?

AARON. How? The walls are paper thin! The guests don't
shut up!

KATHERINE. Excuse me – !

AARON. No! Let me speak! I was terrible at everything,
including sleeping – but then I could *sing*! You must have
heard me sing! She heard me sing!

KATHERINE. Who?

AARON. Her! She knows! She knows that this was real. She
saw what I saw! Then I lost her.

HARD HAT (*low*). This member of your staff should be
escorted to his bed –

AARON. No! I hate the beds here! I work until I'm so tired
I can barely stand, I do everything I'm supposed to do –
I take everybody's crap and so many of those stupid pills but
I can't sleep!

YOLANDA *approaches* AARON. *He's shaking.*

YOLANDA. Pills? What pills?

AARON *produces the pills from his pocket.*

Twelve and a half milligrams of zolpidem – these are strong.
They can… (*Tempering this – concerned for his feelings.*)
cause hallucinations.

AARON *looks up at* YOLANDA.

AARON. Really?

AARON *takes in the faces around the room.*

Just… tell me this – did either of you see her? Or hear her?

KATHERINE. *Who?*

AARON (*tearing up*). I don't know…

I don't know her name!

AARON is about to weep. KATHERINE *and* YOLANDA *each take a side of him. They look concerned –*

Don't take me to that room.

KATHERINE. It's okay… take a seat here.

YOLANDA. You're going to be fine. Give him some space.

Upstage, something is stirring. The door swings –

AMY *is revealed, waking from her concussion. She looks about her, rubbing her sore head. She spots* AARON, *who stares out.*

AARON (*bitterly*). I loved her.

That's the part that felt the most…

That I loved her.

Silence. Deepest silence.

AMY *approaches him.*

At first, she doubts herself – then – decides to go for it.

AMY.
Mon cœur s'ouvre a ta voix
Comme s'ouvrent les fleurs
Aux baisers de l'aurore

[My heart opens to your voice
Like the flowers open
To the kisses of the dawn]

AARON *lifts his head up.*

He whirls around. They stare at each other.

AARON. Are you… a ghost?

AMY. No. I'm a room attendant.

She gently hushes him and walks towards him. Their faces are almost close enough to touch.

AARON. I mean – the tapes? That was – ?

AMY. Me.

AARON. It was.

It was all you.

She nods. They lean closer to one another –

HARD HAT (*uncomfortable*). This is hardly appropriate.

AARON (*astounded*). You see her?

YOLANDA. Of course. (*To* KATHERINE.) I think we should leave them.

HARD HAT. Out of the question. They can't be left up here without my supervision –

KATHERINE. I think that on this one occasion –

HARD HAT. I'm afraid I'm not interested in anyone's workplace romance, boundaries between professional and personal are extremely important to maintain in –

KATHERINE *roughly snogs the* WORKER IN HARD HAT.

KATHERINE. Have a heart you bloody… bore!

The WORKER IN HARD HAT *stares out, incredulous.*

Come on, Yolanda. Let's begin the training downstairs.

All but AARON *and* AMY *exit through the door, which slams shut heavily behind them. We see the staff appear below in the corridor.*

AMY. Did you throw my tapes away?

AARON. No! I treasured them! I wouldn't have survived without them.

AMY. I found the Walkman in the bin.

AARON. I trod on it. It broke my heart.

They look at each other.

I might be very much… mad, you know.

I started to believe that music could bring back the dead.

AMY. Can it not?

Beat.

You can sing.

He doesn't know whether to believe her.

I heard you.

AARON. It scares me.

I go somewhere when I do it.

AMY. Me too. Do you think I'm mad?

AARON. No I think you're wonderful.

She considers kissing him then remembers herself –

AMY. Oh – ! I'm Amy.

AARON. Oh! Aaron.

AMY. How d'you do.

They shake hands, awkward. Then – she looks at him.

I think singing might be what you are for.

They stare at one another.

AARON. I think I'd rather stay up here forever than risk losing you again.

They get closer –

An alarm sounds! Very loud!

AMY. Oh God? What's going on?

AARON. Oh – it's okay. They're just running a fire drill!

AMY. A drill?…We could stay here until it's over?!

They agree. They hold each other.

Lights down on the roof –

Lights up on the corridor –

MORAG *is smoking.* KATHERINE, YOLANDA *and* GENERIC STAFF MEMBER *are stood about.*

MORAG. Oh! What's that?

KATHERINE. That will be the fire drill. Let's evacuate.

MORAG. Right-oh, just a moment –

MORAG *takes a couple more drags on her fag, lest she waste it.*

KATHERINE. Morag, put your cigarette out!

MORAG. What?

KATHERINE. Cig-a-rette?

MORAG. Oh, here you go, Katherine – (*Offering her one.*)

KATHERINE. No – !

MORAG. No, you're alright, honestly – I was aye generous –

KATHERINE. Morag! *Bin.* Everyone – move –

KATHERINE *leads* YOLANDA *and* GENERIC STAFF MEMBER *out of the building –* MORAG *takes a last puff on her cigarette before throwing it in the bin and disappearing.*

Beat.

All at once –

Music. Fire! The bin has caught alight in spectacular fashion and an orchestra has struck up. They are playing the climactic final duet of I Innamorate Fenici.

Lights up on the roof –

AARON. Can you hear that, too?

AMY. Yes. I think I can.

AARON.
> Un sentimento che non potevo contenere
> Condividevo ogni notte con le stelle.

> [A feeling that I could not hold inside me
> I shared each night with the stars.]

AMY.
> Come avrei potuto sapere che per tutta la mia vita
> Stavi cercando di ascoltarmi?

> [How could I have known that all my life
> You were listening out for me?]

GHOSTS OF THE OPERA HOUSE *surround them now –*
this is it. Is that FIGARO, BRÜNNHILDE, CARMEN,
a REGENCY GHOST…

The Phoenician sweethearts are singing their final duet.

The SPIRITS *look on and will the pair to do it beautifully.*

AARON *and* AMY.
> Ora tutt'intorno
> Interi cori cantano

> [Now, all around
> Whole choirs sing]

AARON.
> Dio dipinge bellezza in ogni immagine

> [God paints beauty into every image]

AMY.
> Il divino sconfigge il profano

> [The divine defeats the profane]

AARON *and* AMY.
> Il sublime decora il quotidiano

> [The sublime decorates the mundane]

AMY *and* CHORUS.
  / **Ora tutt'intorno**
  Interi cori cantano

  [Now, all around
  Whole choirs sing]

AARON.
  Ciò che era vuoto è pieno
  E l'insensato, chiaro e vero
  L'inutile, ora prezioso per me

  [What was empty is full
  The senseless, so clear and true
  The worthless, now precious to me]

AMY.
  Adorarti è bruciare

  [To love you is to burn]

AARON.
  Adorarti è bruciare

  [To love you is to burn]

  At that moment, smoke appears.

AMY. Oh, God!

  AARON *tries the door. It will not open.*

AARON. It's stuck!

  Then AMY *tries. It won't budge. She bangs on it –*

AMY. Help!

AARON. Help! Let us out!

AMY. I don't want this for you –

AARON. I don't want it for you – there must be a way down –

AMY. We're too high up!

  Smoke licks at their ankles.

They cling on to each other.

But…

If this is it.

AARON. If we are supposed to… this way…?

AARON *and* AMY. I'll take it.

Music swells. They kiss.

AMY.
Adorarti è bruciare

[To love you is to burn]

AARON.
Adorarti è bruciare

[To love you is to burn]

AARON *and* AMY.
Adorarti è bruciare

[To love you is to burn]

AARON.
Di buon grado

[Willingly]

AMY.
Ora e per sempre

[Now and forever]

AARON.
In queste fiamme

[In this blaze]

AMY.
Di estasi

[Of ecstasy]

AARON.
>**Che rendono**

>**[That makes]**

AMY.
>**Il nostro amore**

>**[Our love]**

AARON.
>**Immortale**

>**[Immortal]**

AMY.
>**Immortale**

>**[Immortal]**

AARON *and* AMY.
>**Immortale**

>**[Immortal]**

>*Passionately they kiss.*

>*Colour! Light!*

>*The* GHOSTS OF THE OPERA *fly into the air and rejoice –
they are free. They take in the young lovers, pleased for
them. They look to one another. It's time. The* GHOSTS *walk
into the fire and disappear.*

>*The music crescendos. The lovers embrace. And in
spectacular fashion it concludes. Rapturous applause from
audiences through the ages. Roses fill the space from all
directions –*

>*All settles. The lovers intertwined, as one. Engulfed by
smoke.*

>*Peace.*

>*A head appears – smoking a cigarette.*

MORAG. You two nutcases coming down the fire escape? The
hotel's a gonner!

AARON. Morag – ! How did you get it open?

MORAG. Ach, it's like anything…

There's a knack to it.

The End.

A Nick Hern Book

The Grand Old Opera House Hotel first published as a paperback original in Great Britain in 2023 by Nick Hern Books Limited, The Glasshouse, 49a Goldhawk Road, London W12 8QP, in association with the Traverse Theatre and Dundee Rep

Cover design: design:**feast**creative.com

Designed and typeset by Nick Hern Books, London
Printed in Great Britain by Mimeo Ltd, Huntingdon, Cambridgeshire PE29 6XX

A CIP catalogue record for this book is available from the British Library

ISBN   978 1 83904 272 0

www.nickhernbooks.co.uk/environmental-policy